SELF-ESTEEM ENHANCEMENT WITH CHILDREN AND ADOLESCENTS

Titles of Related Interest

Cartledge/Milburn TEACHING SOCIAL SKILLS TO CHILDREN:
Innovative Approaches, Second Edition
Johnson/Rasbury/Siegel APPROACHES TO CHILD TREATMENT:
Introduction to Theory, Research and Practice
Matson/Ollendick ENHANCING CHILDREN'S SOCIAL SKILLS:
Assessment and Training
Morris/Kratochwill THE PRACTICE OF CHILD THERAPY
Oster/Caro/Eagen/Lillo ASSESSING ADOLESCENTS
Schwartz/Johnson PSYCHOPATHOLOGY OF CHILDHOOD:
A Clinical Experimental Approach, Second Edition

Related Journals

CHILD ABUSE AND NEGLECT
CLINICAL PSYCHOLOGY REVIEW
JOURNAL OF CHILD PSYCHOLOGY AND PSYCHIATRY
AND ALLIED DISCIPLINES

PSYCHOLOGY PRACTITIONER GUIDEBOOKS

EDITORS

Arnold P. Goldstein, Syracuse University
Leonard Krasner, Stanford University & SUNY at Stony Brook
Sol L. Garfield, Washington University in St. Louis

SELF-ESTEEM ENHANCEMENT WITH CHILDREN AND ADOLESCENTS

ALICE W. POPE
SUSAN M. McHALE
The Pennsylvania State University

W. EDWARD CRAIGHEAD
Duke University Medical Center

ALLYN AND BACON
Boston London Toronto Sydney Tokyo Singapore

Printed in the United States of America

10 9 8 7 6 5 4   96

ISBN 0-205-14455-1

Library of Congress Cataloging in Publication Data
Pope, Alice W.
Self-esteem enhancement with children and adolescents/ Alice
W. Pope, Susan M. McHale, W. Edward Craighead.
p.   cm. – (Psychology practitioner guidebooks)
Bibliography: p.
Includes index.
1. Self-respect in children. 2. Self-respect in teenagers.
3. Cognitive therapy. I. McHale, Susan. II. Craighead,
W. Edward. III. Title. IV. Series.
RJ506.L68P66 1988   618.92'8914-dc19   87-36885

Printed in Great Britain by Richard Clay Ltd. Bungay, Suffolk

Contents

Preface

The treatment program presented in this book was initially developed in response to a request for help from an elementary school principal. The school had just received the results from yearly statewide achievement tests, and although the academic scores were satisfactory, results from a self-esteem test were alarming. The findings indicated that some of the school's most talented and intellectually gifted students were evaluating themselves quite negatively. How could this be, wondered the principal, when the academic success of these children was so outstanding? Clearly, something needed to be done, but what? At this point, the principal contacted one of the authors to help address that school's particular problem. Another of the authors became involved in the development of the treatment aspects of that program, which became the basis of this manual. Another person became involved in the development of this program as we attempted to revise it for use with handicapped children. Its final development resulted from utilizing these procedures in the treatment of low self-esteem children in an outpatient clinical setting.

Two interesting conclusions emerged from this experience. First, it became apparent that a child's self-esteem may be very discrepant from an objective assessment of his skills and abilities. The school children who were the initial recipients of this treatment program were able to accurately identify and describe their areas of strength, yet were not particularly impressed. Their standards for themselves were so high that in spite of their truly exceptional abilities, they seldom saw their efforts as "good enough." In fact, they believed that possessing unusual talents justified these extremely high standards. Given this approach to self-evaluation, the utility of cognitive-behavioral interventions seemed clear. In regard to their areas of strength, these children needed to learn the cognitive skills in order to evaluate themselves differently, in a way which provided for a more realistic and self-enhancing attitude. The children also had some weak areas, mostly concerning peer relationships. Here their negative self-view was more accurate, since they did indeed lack some age-appropriate social skills. However, the emphasis they placed on "failures" in the social arena was disproportionate and distorted. Interventions involved training in communication skills (a focus on behavior) and in a number of new strategies for evaluating self-performance (a focus on cognition). These examples demonstrated the lack of correspondence which may occur between a child's actual abilities and her evaluation of these abilities, and they point to interventions targeting both behaviors and cognitions, in order to have an effective impact on self-esteem.

Once developed and implemented this self-esteem enhancement program attracted widespread interest. Professionals who work with children are often very concerned with obvious low self-esteem in a child, yet are frustrated when trying to work with such an elusive construct as self-esteem; many have told us of their desire to find a structured treatment program. At the policy and planning level, state governments, along with the National Education Association, are looking for ways to implement programs which instill positive self-images in school children (New Options, 1986). However, although many people agree that helping children to achieve healthy self-esteem is worthwhile, knowing how to put that idea into practice is another matter. Self-esteem is, simply, a very complex entity.

We dealt with that complexity by using an approach that divides self-esteem into its component pieces and then intervenes from multiple perspectives. For example, in addition to global, overall self-esteem, we look at self-esteem as it relates to body image, peer relations, and other areas corresponding to the developmental level and individual needs of the child. Once areas of strengths and weaknesses are identified, we use interventions which target the cognitions, emotions, and behaviors associated with weaker areas, while emphasizing the strengths. The intervention strategies are based upon cognitive–behavioral techniques, which have previously been used successfully to help children, adolescents, and adults change the way they think, feel, and act. What is unique about this program is that these techniques have been organized into a comprehensive treatment package designed to take the child's developmental level into account in attempting to enhance self-esteem. It is our hope that this program will be useful to professionals who work with children and adolescents—in schools, hospitals, social service agencies, and private practice.

Chapter 1

Self-esteem: An Introduction

The importance of self-esteem has consistently been appreciated by those who work with children. It is difficult to have close contact with children and avoid being concerned with their most central feelings about themselves as individuals. Recently, it seems that self-esteem has become an increasingly popular topic; books for parents, teachers, counselors, and for children themselves stress the need for "positive self-esteem." Educational systems are also becoming involved. Schools are beginning to assume responsibility for teaching children that they are worthwhile, often employing standardized self-esteem testing and classroom curricula aimed at enhancing feelings of self-worth. Programs such as these have generated many questions about how to work with children who have self-esteem problems.

It is easy to become confused when thinking about children's self-esteem. The language used can be unclear, with "self-esteem" and "self-concept" often used interchangeably. The cause and effect dynamics are difficult to understand; does low self-esteem cause other problems in children's lives, or do these problems themselves contribute to a shaky sense of self-worth? In practice, it can be hard to identify children who are having trouble with self-esteem. The most frustrating question is: What can be done to help children suffering from low self-esteem? This chapter will attempt to clarify some of these issues by introducing the reader to the perspective taken by the authors. The model presented here in chapter 1 represents a basic view of self-esteem, while chapter 3 will further elaborate this model and discuss ways in which it varies developmentally.

WHAT IS SELF-ESTEEM?

Self-esteem can be differentiated from self-concept, which is the constellation of things a person uses to describe himself. A child might see himself as a good baseball player, Joe's friend, a person interested in science fiction, an average student—these would be components of his *self-concept*. *Self-esteem* is an *evaluation* of the information contained in the self-concept, and is derived from a child's feelings about *all* the things he is. If a child places a high value on being a superior student but is himself only an average or poor student, his self-esteem will suffer. The same child, however, could value athletic ability and popularity over academic ability, and consequently have a high self-esteem if he is accomplished in the first two areas. An individual's self-esteem, then, is based upon a combination of objective information about oneself and subjective evaluation of that information.

We can examine the formation of self-esteem by thinking about the *perceived self* and the *ideal self*. The perceived self is the same as self-concept—an objective view of those skills, characteristics and qualities which are present and absent. The ideal self is an image of the person one would like to be—not in a frivolous manner (I wish I were a millionaire; I'd like to be a famous movie star) but rather a sincere desire to possess certain attributes. When the perceived and ideal selves are a good match, the self-esteem will be positive. For example, a child who values academic success and is a good student will feel good about himself; he has a positive evaluation of his actual characteristics. Conversely, a child whose ideal self is to be very popular but who in actuality has few friends will have low self-esteem. It is the discrepancy between perceived self and ideal self that leads to problems with self-esteem.

What, then, is meant by "high" or "low" self-esteem? A high self-esteem is considered to be a "healthy" view of the self—one that realistically encompasses shortcomings but is not harshly critical of them. A person who has a positive self-esteem evaluates herself in a positive way and feels good about her strong points. Feeling satisfied with major portions of the self does not mean that the individual has no desire to be different in any way; on the contrary, a self-confident person often works hard at improving weak areas, yet is forgiving of herself when at times she falls short of her goals.

Someone with a low self-esteem frequently exhibits an artificially positive self-attitude to the world, in a desperate attempt to prove to others— and herself—that she is an adequate person. Or she may retreat into herself, fearing contact with others who, she fears, will ultimately reject her. A person with low self-esteem is essentially a person who finds little to be proud of in herself.

Low self-esteem can be less far-reaching if only a few areas of the self are affected. The self-concept, and consequently self-esteem, are made up of many components which come from the things in our lives that are important to us. For example, the child mentioned earlier gave evaluations of himself in the areas of athletics, friendships, interests, and academics. His overall, or global, self-esteem will depend on the importance he gives to each of the components—essentially, if he values the areas he feels good about, his global self-esteem will be positive, while a devaluation of those areas will result in negative feelings about himself as a whole. Some children do not appreciate any of their own good qualities or abilities, instead placing a high value on all the things they do not do as well. These children will obviously have more difficulty with their global self-esteem than those who acknowledge their strengths.

Each person values different things about himself. William James (1890) beautifully expressed this idea:

> I, who for the time have staked my all on being a psychologist, am mortified if others know much more psychology than I. But I am contented to wallow in the grossest ignorance of Greek. My deficiencies there give me no sense of personal humiliation at all. Had I "pretensions" to be a linguist, it would have been just the reverse (p. 309).

Children, however, tend to be fairly similar to each other in terms of which areas they value about themselves. This is due, in part, to the structure of their lives (they all must go to school; most live in families) and to the developmental tasks facing them (they are learning to get along with others, and are discovering the changing capabilities and appearances of their bodies). Therefore, it is often useful to look at a child's self-esteem in five areas: social, academic, family, body image, and global self-esteem.

The *social* area encompasses the child's feelings about himself as a friend to others. Do other children like him, value his ideas, include him in their activities? Does he feel satisfied with his interactions and relationships with peers? A child whose social needs are being met (regardless of how well they match up to traditional conceptions of "popularity") will feel comfortable with this aspect of himself.

The *academic* area deals with the child's evaluation of himself as a student. This is not simply an assessment of academic ability and achievement—not all children can be "A" students! Instead, this is an instance where the child decides if he is "good enough." If he meets his own standards for academic achievement (and naturally these standards are shaped by family, friends, and teachers), then his academic self-esteem will be positive.

The *family* self-esteem reflects his feelings about himself as a member of his family. A child who feels he is a valued member of his family, who makes his own unique contribution, and who is secure in the love and respect he receives from parents and siblings, will have a highly positive self-esteem in this area.

Body image is a combination of physical appearances and capabilities. The child's self-esteem in this area is based upon his satisfaction with the way his body looks and performs. Typically, girls have been more concerned with appearance and boys with athletic ability, but this is not necessarily the case for individual children, and traditional roles are changing for today's children.

The *global* self-esteem is a more general appraisal of the self, and, as we saw earlier, is based on the child's evaluation of all parts of himself. A positive global self-esteem would be reflected in feelings such as "I'm a good person" or "I like most things about myself."

To summarize, then, self-esteem arises from the discrepancy between the perceived self, or self-concept (an objective view of the self and the ideal self (what the person values, or wants to be like). A large discrepancy results in low self-esteem, while a small discrepancy is usually indicative of high self-esteem. This sort of "measuring up" occurs in many areas of life, depending upon the types of endeavors and interests in which the person is engaged. If we are interested in changing a person's self-esteem, we have several approaches to take. First, we can focus on a particular area which is problematic (i.e., academic, family, and so forth). Second, we can look at the discrepancy between perceived and ideal selves. To modify the discrepancy, we can work from either end: we can help the person to change his or her ideal self so that he is better able to achieve his goals, or we can help him to change his perceived self so that he can see himself more positively (although the perceived self is often described as objective, it is subject to distortions, and is sometimes very negatively biased). We can also consider teaching the child skills which will improve his actual performance in a particular area. The approach taken with each individual will vary according to his needs, but these are the points of intervention which potentially are available.

WHY IS SELF-ESTEEM IMPORTANT?

Most practitioners view positive self-esteem as a central factor in good social-emotional adjustment. This view is widespread, and has a long history. Early psychologists and sociologists, such as William James, George Herbert Mead, and Charles Cooley, were among the first to stress the importance of a positive self-esteem. Years later, the neo-Freudians—

among them Adler, Sullivan, and Horney—incorporated the self-concept into their theories of personality, as did Rogers and Fromm. More recently, scientific psychologists have combined theory with empirical work to conclude that positive self-esteem is related to happier and more effective functioning; for example, depression has been linked to a cognitive style that includes excessively critical and negative evaluations of the self.

For children, a healthy self-esteem has been seen as especially valuable, since it serves as the foundation for a child's perceptions of life experiences. The social–emotional competence derived from this positive self-appraisal can be a force that helps the child avoid future serious problems. Evidence for this viewpoint can be seen in the *Diagnostic and Statistical Manual of Mental Disorders* (American Psychiatric Association, 1987), which contains the criteria most frequently used in this country for making psychiatric diagnoses. Low self-esteem is mentioned as an associated feature of several of the childhood disorders. Two very different examples of this are attention deficit disorder, which is marked by impulsivity and inattention (these children are commonly called "hyperactive"), and avoidant disorder, a severe form of social anxiety. Although it is unclear whether low self-esteem actually is a cause of any disorder, the fact that it can be associated with serious problems in childhood may be reason enough to intervene. In any case, it seems plausible that a strong self-esteem could, to some extent, offset some childhood problems, resulting in difficulties of a less severe nature. A child who feels good about herself may cope better with the problems she encounters so that they never develop into major difficulties for her.

In addition to being a component of mental health, self-esteem appears to be associated with academic achievement. Numerous researchers have found a relationship between positive self-esteem and higher grades in school. This relationship is even stronger when one looks specifically at children's evaluations of themselves as students, which could be called their "academic self-esteem." Again, we can't be certain whether high self-esteem *causes* good grades or vice versa, but causality probably operates in both directions. A child's view of his or her academic performance will certainly affect his self-evaluation. Conversely, a phenomenon known as a "self-fulfilling prophecy" suggests that an individual's beliefs about himself will have a strong impact on how well he performs, sometimes in spite of his actual abilities.

To summarize, self-esteem is an important aspect of a child's overall functioning. It appears to be related to other areas, including psychological health and academic performance, in an interactional manner; that is, self-esteem may be both a cause and an effect of the type of functioning which occurs in other areas. Because of this interactional relationship

between self-esteem and other areas, it is important to direct interventions at several different domains of the self, as will be described in
chapter 2.

HOW DO YOU KNOW IF A CHILD
HAS LOW SELF-ESTEEM?

In reality, there is no way to know for sure if a child has low self-
esteem, any more than one ever truly knows the content of children's
thoughts and feelings. To arrive at a "best guess," professional judgment
must be made on the basis of interviews with the child, his parents, and
his teachers; observation of the child in different settings; and perhaps
the use of a self-esteem test administered to the child. A complete
description of the assessment of self-esteem in a child can be found in
chapter 4.

THE ETHICS OF CHANGE

It is important for all practitioners to give some thought to the issues
surrounding the treatment of low self-esteem in children. This is one
situation where the child's wishes must ultimately be respected; no counselor can make these decisions for the child. When working with self-
esteem, the basic questions concern choices about the type of person the
child will be—what his values will be, what goals he will aspire to, which
dreams he will put aside. While thoughtful guidance can be very useful
to the child, it is essential to realize that we must respect the child's
decisions and not impose our own values on him.

Chapter 2

The Social Learning Model

The model from which we derived procedures to enhance self-esteem is labeled a social learning model. The basic assumption of the social learning model is that self-esteem enhancement procedures are best developed from the findings of basic psychology research. In order to make these findings more useful, they are grouped into the following domains: *behavioral, cognitive, biological,* and *emotional.* Examples of behavior would include social skills such as giving compliments, smiling, talking and so on. Examples of cognition would be self-statements, imaging, beliefs, and fantasies. Biological variables relevant to self-esteem include physical size and specific deficits such as a handicapping condition; the relationship of biological development to age is also important. Emotions—labeled as "feelings" in everyday vernacular—play a significant role in self-esteem. As noted in chapter 1, individual evaluations of self-concept determine the balance of the feelings in self-esteem.

These variables are related to self-esteem in the following way. A youngster uses what he does, how he behaves (his behavioral repertoire) to describe himself in his self-concept. Thus, a boy who has good skills for catching a baseball and hitting it with a bat will very likely describe himself as a good baseball player. If he plays on a regular basis with another boy about his age, named Joe, he will probably describe himself as Joe's friend. In other words his self-concept, the constellation of things he uses to describe himself, is based on his own behavior. Each behavior can become a part of the self-concept. Since self-esteem is an evaluation of the self-concept, one method of changing self-esteem is to change the behavioral repertoire on which the evaluated self-concept is based. How does one change behavior, or how is a new behavior learned?

At the most basic level, behavior is changed according to some principles derived from the area of psychology called *learning theory.* Since the focus is on social development, the utilization of these principles in

7

applied settings such as home and school is called *social learning*. These basic principles have been known for some time and sometimes are taken for granted, so it is desirable for us to briefly review them. In order for a behavior to increase it should be followed by reinforcement: either the application of a positive reinforcer, or termination of a negative re-inforcer. For example, you receive money for your work; the money is a positive reinforcer, and you continue to work in order to get more of it. A whining child is a master user of negative reinforcers. We engage in various conciliatory behavior in order to get the child to stop whining. The behaviors that work on one occasion are likely to occur on the next occasion because that behavior resulted in a termination of the child's whining, which serves as negative reinforcement.

In order to decrease a behavior, the behavior should be followed by punishment: either the application of an aversive stimulus, such as a reprimand, or the termination of a positive stimulus, such as a TV pro-gram. In other words, a child is likely to decrease a behavior which is quickly and consistently followed by a verbal reprimand from another person, e.g. a teacher. An alternative method of decreasing a behavior would be to follow the behavior with the termination of a positive stimulus, such as turning off a TV program or removing a dessert.

	Applied	Removed
Reinforcer	Positive reinforcement	Punishment by removal
Punisher	Punishment by application	Negative reinforcement

FIGURE 2.1. Basic principles of learning.

Another way to decrease the frequency of a behavior is *extinction*. This means that a behavior previously followed by a reinforcer is no longer followed by a reinforcer. When a previously reinforced behavior is no longer reinforced, it often increases in frequency at first but it gradually decreases. For example, whining is frequently attended to by a parent; this attention frequently is in the form of telling the child to "stop whining." In fact, the parent's attention is reinforcing the very behavior the parent does not want to occur. If the parent decides to totally ignore the child's whining, the frequency and perhaps volume of whining will increase at first and then gradually decrease. It is important to understand this pattern, because many parents will conclude that extinction is not occurring when the behavior first increases, and consequently will abort the program and revert to the "stop whining" *reinforcement* at the very worst time, i.e., at the time the undesired behavior has increased. Thus, if an extinction program is begun the parent must understand how it works and be prepared to stick it out until the extinction occurs. Although the behavior usually decreases more slowly with extinction than it does with punishment, many people prefer to use this process because it does not have the adverse connotations associated with punishment.

The teacher may also use other findings from learning research. For example, the principle of *shaping* is important in teaching a new behavior. In shaping, you reinforce responses similar to the target behavior. As the child gradually approximates the target behavior, reinforcement is only given for those responses which are gradually more similar to the target toward which the behavior is moving. In other words, the teacher only reinforces those responses which move from where the child begins to the final goal behavior. This requires the teacher to either define the criteria for the steps to be reinforced or to make judgments about how closely the behavior resembles the target behavior. For example, in teaching a child to make letters of the alphabet, you would at first praise any attempt at moving the pencil to make the marks on the paper. Gradually, however, you would only praise those marks which more closely approximate the actual letter you are teaching the child to draw.

Another finding important in learning is the role of *instructions*. A teacher may use clear instructions to describe the appropriate behavior and its contingent relationship to the positive or negative stimulus which will follow it. It is important to ensure that the instructions are understood by the child. They must be given at the age-appropriate level.

Another basic aspect of learning comes from the observational learning data. Learning is facilitated by someone demonstrating the target behavior; this holds for verbal behavior as well as somatic–motor or gross motor responses. If the modeled, or demonstrated, behavior is followed by an appropriate consequence, the behavior is more readily imitated by the child who is learning. Videotaped modeling has been used effectively to teach children new responses. Another child who knows a coping, adaptive response may demonstrate it on a videotape. Modeling effectiveness can be enhanced by using a model similar to the youngster and by assuring that the model demonstrates how the modeled behavior fits the response needed by the child who is learning. In other words, child one shows child two how it works.

Modeling new behaviors and presenting positive reinforcement, such as complimenting appropriate behavior, are essential ingredients toward changing the behavior on which the self-concept is based. Take, for example, communication skills with peers at school. A fundamental communication skill is understanding the feelings expressed by another child as part of a conversation. First, it is important to instruct the child about the target behavior, namely, listening to the friend and communicating that she understands what the friend is feeling. To do that, a child must listen to *all* of what a friend says and then respond with an appropriate comment or question. This can be modeled in conversation with the child by observing what the child feels and demonstrating your understanding through use of relevant questions. Videotapes of successful models utilizing good conversation skills can be effectively employed. Once the child imitates the model and responds appropriately to the feelings expressed in the conversation, she should be verbally praised (complimented) for engaging in the newly acquired behavior. Once this new communication skill is learned, it can serve as the basis for the development of other socially skillful behaviors.

Various other behavior skills can be taught by the effective use of these principles of learning. It is important, as we shall see in the next chapter, that the expected appropriate behaviors and the reinforcers and punishers be geared to the developmental level of the child.

Learning always occurs in some environmental context. Some environments are more conducive to learning than others. You should work in a setting that will allow the child to learn new behaviors while she is free from the distraction of other children or activities. On the other hand, the new behavior is likely to be used in situations most similar to the one in which it is learned, so it is desirable to work in a setting as close and similar to "real life" as possible.

These techniques are essential to the basic enhancement of self-esteem. Many times self-esteem cannot go up without a prior change in self-concept, which is based on the behavioral repertoire of the child. Certain behaviors are essential to subsequent changes in self-esteem because they are necessary for other, subsequent behaviors. For example, a child cannot successfully give someone a compliment unless he possesses basic communications skills and can identify the perspective of another. If you do not know what is important to the other person, it is difficult to give a compliment that sounds sincere. Thus, some thought must go into the planning and sequencing of behavioral repertoires. A child must possess the prerequisite behaviors for each new behavior that is to be taught.

As is clear from chapter 1, however, high self-esteem is based on a positive evaluation of the self concept and how well the *perceived* self-concept matches the *ideal* self-concept. The perceived self-concept is a *cognitive* activity of the child. It is not just what we do, but what we *think* we do that affects our perceptions. Changing the perceived self-concept is a cognitive activity. There are some principles from cognitive psychology that are useful for facilitating cognitive change.

One of the basic findings of cognitive psychology is that humans possess problem-solving skills. The potential discrepancy between our ideal and perceived self-concepts can be viewed as a problem to be solved. This includes the adoption of a problem-solving set and the definition of the problem which needs solving. A third step in the solving of problems is the generation of alternative solutions, and implementation of the most desirable alternative. This procedure was described in some detail by D'Zurilla and Goldfried (1971). It allows us to decide what behaviors need to be learned and to define how they will fit within a self-concept. Furthermore, the cognitive activity of problem solving may allow the child to identify problems among her other cognitive activities. For example, the child may discover that she evaluates her self-concept too negatively because she has been evaluating it against too high a standard. This may result in the depression and feelings of worthlessness which accompany low self-esteem. The identified problem now is a cognitive one—high standard setting—and the child needs to develop solutions to solve this cognitive problem. The cognitive problem-solving procedures are described in detail in chapter 5, and the specifics of the modification of standard setting are spelled out in chapter 9.

There are a number of other cognitive distortions which may occur in our thinking and evaluation of the self-concept. These distortions contribute to inappropriate low self-esteem, and when this is the problem the solution is a correction of the cognitive distortions and not a change in the behavioral repertoire. Sacco and Beck (1985) have listed the following distortions which occur in self-statements or thoughts:

1. arbitrary inference—drawing conclusions without data or with contrary data
2. selective abstraction—focusing on a negative detail
3. overgeneralization—drawing conclusions on the basis of one incident
4. magnification—overestimating negative events
   minification—underestimating positive events
5. personalization—an attributional style which takes personal responsibility for negative events
6. dichotomous thinking—all-or-none thinking

These types of distortions are especially relevant to low self-esteem. If they occur in the process of constructing the self-concept, they only leave room for negative self-esteem. The cognitive model assumes that these cognitive errors affect how you subsequently feel about yourself, and, in a cognitive fashion, come around to influence how you behave. In other words, how you think affects how you act.

Other psychologists, most notably Zajonc (1980), have argued that feelings may indeed precede thoughts, and that how you feel about yourself influences how you think and behave. In other words, your feelings play a causative role in how you think and behave. Undoubtedly, some feelings seem to occur and influence behavior before you have time to think about them.

At the same time biological processes must be taken into account in several ways. At one level all of behavior can be reduced to biological responses. Signals are perceived via a biological process, be it seeing or hearing; at the same time, perceiving is usually labeled a cognitive process. It seems that the most parsimonious way to think of these processes is that they occur simultaneously and are reciprocally interdependent on one another. A biological perception means very little to a human being unless it has meaning attached to it via a cognitive process.

The cognitive-behavioral model (see Craighead, Meyers, & Craighead, 1985) then posits the following dimensions. There is an environment, or setting, in which events occur; for purposes of the topic of self-esteem, these settings include, primarily, the home, the family, and the school with classmates and teachers. The school is both an academic and a social setting. There are also person variables relevant to self-esteem. These person variables can occur simultaneously, at any point in time, and can also influence each other from time 1 to time 2. The model on page 13 demonstrates the directions of influence.

It doesn't really matter which comes first because there is a reciprocal interdependence, which means that every person variable affects every other person variable. Furthermore, you can intervene effectively in any of the four person domains or even in the environmental domain. As we saw earlier, an environmental intervention is especially effective in changing behavior (i.e., the use of reinforcement). Perhaps the most direct and effective intervention is one which involves correction in the domain in which the problem is occurring. Thus, one uses the overall problem-solving strategy (see chapter 5) to identify the problem domain. Then one intervenes directly in that domain. So if a cognitive error is identified, then one does cognitive interventions to correct it; these processes are discussed in chapters 6–9. If one identifies a behavioral deficiency, a behavior modification program is undertaken to teach the needed behavior—e.g. communication skills, as discussed in chapter 11. If there is a problem in the emotional area, then attempts are made to intervene directly on emotional functioning. Emotions exist on their own—all people, including children, have feelings. However, not all people are equally adept at labeling and identifying their feeling states. Children need to learn labels for their feelings in order to understand

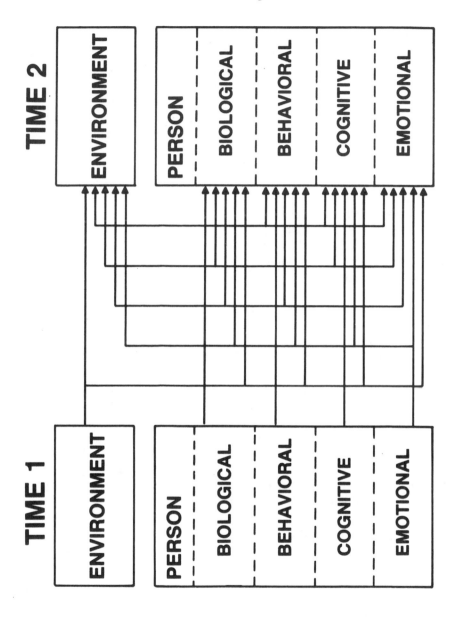

themselves adequately, to understand others' feelings, and to communicate with others by reflecting others' feelings and by expressing
their own feelings. Although psychologists and counselors are limited in
the area of biological interventions, there are a number of areas for work;
these include exercise, eating habits, and sleep habits. Of course personal

cognitive interpretations regarding size and development have a biological basis, discussed in chapter 12. Accepting one's body in the developmental process is an important component of self-esteem. Western cultures, including the U.S., go to great extremes to make every conceivable effort to make self-presentation better. The efforts range from tanning salons to diets of every variety. Body image probably plays its biggest role at school transition points: e.g., in junior high school, the early developing girls and the late developing boys show the greatest reductions in self-esteem between grades 6 and grades 7 (see Simons & Blyth, in press).

Enhancing self-esteem is accomplished by improving one or more of these domains within the individual. Errors have been made in previous programs, which focus on enhancing an abstract concept called "self-esteem." You cannot directly enhance self-esteem, but you can indirectly affect it by changing one or more of the person variables—behavior, cognition, emotion, or biology. This program works on all four domains in a developmental framework. For example, you cannot teach the cognitive skill of understanding another person's emotional perspective until the child knows what his own feelings are. A student cannot understand the response of others in conversational interactions unless the basic communication skills are in place and others' feelings can be understood. Recognition and acknowledgement of the other person's feelings is crucial to the successful use of communication skills.

This program assumes that a child is developing in all four domains. Development, however, does not occur in a synchrony across all domains. Therefore, a child may develop faster in one domain than in another. An obvious example of this dysynchrony in development is the child who has grown physically but has not kept up in the psychological domains of cognition and emotion. The thinking and feeling have not kept up with biological development, so the child may not understand the biological functions and drives of his or her body.

The purpose of this program, as it alternately focuses on development within and across the person domains, is to provide the stimulus for arranging synchrony across the domains. It provides the necessary "growth spurts" to those domains lagging behind in development. The next chapter describes those developmental processes. Following a brief discussion of how to use the manual, we will discuss, in detail, an intervention in various domains within a developmental framework.

Chapter 3
Developmental Characteristics

Adults who have spent time with children of different ages know that it takes different experiences to make preschoolers, grade school children, and adolescents feel good about themselves. The attention and responsiveness of adults may be more important to a three-year-old learning a new skill than the actual quality of her task performance. In contrast, a nine-year-old may be so concerned about getting a job done correctly that positive adult attention may be an ineffective substitute for task failure. The socially sensitive adolescent counts on both parents and peers for approval and information about her competencies, but her newfound capacity for introspection means that she may interpret social feedback in ways that others do not intend; that is, what she thinks about herself may cause her to distort feedback given by others.

Thus far we have discussed self-esteem as though its causes and manifestations were fairly constant across development. Because the treatment approach described here is targeted toward a particular age group, we have felt safe adopting such a strategy. Youngsters develop at very different rates, however, and consequently, it is important for the practitioner to know just where the school-age child's self-esteem has come from (developmentally speaking) and where it is going.

In this chapter we discuss three major components of what Susan Harter (1983) has termed "the self system": self-concept, self-control, and self-esteem. This model of the self represents an elaboration of the basic scheme we described in chapter 1. We will examine how these aspects of the self are related to one another and how each changes as children mature. In addition, we will briefly explore some ideas about the causes of differences between children in each of these components of the self system. We will then turn to a consideration of how children's developmental status should influence the practitioner's choice of assessment and treatment strategies.

We focus on age differences in this chapter, but it is important to remember that differences in age or rate of development are not the only important differences between children that might affect their self-esteem and their responsiveness to treatment. Certainly boys and girls and children from different ethnic or social class backgrounds may have different reasons for self-esteem problems and may respond to treatment in different ways; the sensitive practitioner will recognize and attend to these differences. *We hope that some of the considerations we raise here regarding developmental differences will be applied to other kinds of individual differences as well.*

THE SELF SYSTEM

A child's self-concept (her views of what she is like) and her self-control abilities (the extent to which she directs the course of her own behavior and activities), in combination with her feelings of self-esteem, make up the self system (Harter, 1983). In recent years researchers have become interested in how these aspects of the self are related to one another and in how each is formed and subsequently changes as a child matures. Unfortunately, the field still has a long way to go in answering these questions. In the following pages, however, we discuss what is known about these components of the self, and we also offer some speculations about the linkages among them.

Self-Concept

As we noted in chapter 1, William James, writing in the late 1800s, proposed that self-esteem could be defined as the relationship between a person's actual self and his ideal self: To the extent that the "real" self fails to meet the standards of the "ideal" self, a person will experience low self-esteem. The question that arises given this point of view is how an individual develops ideas about what his "real" self is. Developmental psychologists have wondered: (a) what are the causes of differences between individuals' self-concepts; and (b) how does the self-concept change developmentally?

In regard to the first question, a number of possible sources for children's self-concepts have been proposed. A group of social psychologists who describe themselves as "symbolic interactionists" believe that individuals develop an idea about who they are based on how they are treated or seen by others (e.g., Cooley, 1902; Mead, 1934). This view of the self has been called the "looking glass self" to emphasize the point that what we think we are is a mirror reflection of how others see us. Thus, a child who is told she is a "naughty child," who is attended to only when she is misbehaving, and whose interactions with adults usually involve disciplinary attempts will come to see herself as a "bad girl." Similarly, children may come to see themselves as bright or dull, feminine or masculine, sickly or healthy. More importantly, once children develop ideas about who they are, they may begin to behave more often in ways that are consistent with their self-concepts, and, in turn, receive feedback from others that supports their ideas about what they are like. In this way, others' views become *self-fulfilling prophecies* about a child's self-concept.

The process of self-concept formation does not always result in a negative self-image. For instance, one view holds that children establish stable gender identities—or ideas about their maleness or femaleness—in the same way they develop other parts of their self-concept (Kohlberg, 1966). Once children come to see themselves as boys or girls, they begin to search for additional characteristics of males or females which they then can adopt. For instance, they may view the behavior of adults and other children or media protrayals of males and females and attempt to behave accordingly. In this way they further define themselves in accordance with one sex or another. As anyone who has worked with young children knows, however, what little boys see as masculine (playing with trucks and "action figures") and little girls see as feminine (playing with carriages and dolls) are very different from school age children's, adolescents', or adults' concepts of masculinity and femininity. In fact, children's ideas about many of their own and others' personal characteristics seem to change in fairly systematic ways as they grow up (Livesley & Bromley, 1973).

One very important change is that children attend to increasingly more abstract personal qualities as they mature. Researchers who study infants' "ideas" about the self, for example, focus on whether a baby can recognize herself (in a mirror or in a photograph) or whether she can discriminate between the environmental consequences of her own actions versus those of someone else (Flavell, 1985). In infancy, then, the sense of self is limited to the *physical* self and the immediate effects of *physical* movements. This self-conception is acquired over the first one to two years of life, as the infant begins to separate herself and her own actions from other objects in the social and physical environments.

When children first begin to describe themselves using words, we see that their self-concepts are still limited to very concrete characteristics. Thus, a preschooler might describe his physical appearance or his possessions when describing himself (e.g., "I have brown hair and a red bicycle"). It is only during grade school that children begin to use trait-like terms ("nice," "friendly") to describe themselves. Even here, how-ever, we see a developmental progression in the kinds of labels children use. From the school age years to young adulthood, individuals move from using terms to describe their *characters* (honest, neat) and *emotional attributes and control* (happy, bad-tempered) to using labels describing *interpersonal traits* (friendly, shy, popular) and finally to terms describing their *psychological makeups* (i.e., their attitudes, values, beliefs). On a more general level, the nature of individuals' self-concepts can be seen as developing from ideas about the bodily self, to the *inner* or *moral* self (Epstein, 1973; Harter, 1983; Livesley & Bromley, 1973; Peevers & Secord, 1973; Rosenberg, 1979).

For practitioners interested in changing children's evaluations of them-selves, knowing just where a child is on this continuum will make a difference in terms of what dimensions of the self-concept are targeted, and, perhaps, in terms of what intervention strategies are employed. For instance, a grade school child who describes herself in interpersonal terms may require help in better understanding the viewpoints of others and in resolving interpersonal problems when she suffers from low self-esteem. A youngster who is more developmentally advanced, who thinks about himself in terms of his attitudes and values, may benefit more from working on appropriate standard setting when *he* manifests low self-esteem. In chapter 10, we discuss more completely the ways in which youngsters' cognitive development affects their social understand-ing, and in turn their self-esteem.

Children's cognitive skills affect their concepts of themselves in other ways as well. For instance, with development children's concepts become increasingly differentiated. Young childen are apt to describe themselves in an absolute, either–or fashion ("I'm either nice *or* I'm mean"; "I'm either honest *or* a liar"). When their concepts are absolute, young children may be particularly subject to self-esteem problems. That is, a single experience with failure or criticism may lead the child to believe he is (completely) "bad." On the other hand, because of their absolutist think-ing, young children also may deny that they ever exhibit any negative characteristics or behavior. Thus, a child who sees herself in a positive light may claim with sincerity that she never lies and she is always polite (Harter, 1983; Livesley & Bromley, 1973).

As children grow older they begin to understand, first, that they can be different at different times ("Sometimes I lie, mostly I tell the truth"), and second, that the same characteristic or behavior can have both posi-tive and negative dimensions ("When I told the truth Mom thought I did the right thing but my brother thought I was a tattle-tale"). Older children may have a fairly easy time recognizing that dispositional (happy, sad) or even interpersonal (friendly, kind) qualities are not absolute; however, a great deal of cognitive sophistication is required before such differentiation can be applied at the level of the "moral self." Even for adults it may be difficult to comprehend that "a" bigot, "a" chauvinist, "a" communist or "a" murderer is not necessarily a completely bad person.

As children move from concrete and absolute to increasingly abstract and differentiated conceptions of the self, age-related changes in children's understanding of the social world also affect the shaping of their self-concepts. From the preschool to the school age years, for instance, children become more oriented to the opinions and perspectives of others around them, in part because they are better able to understand points of view that differ from their own (Flavell, 1985). This awareness leads children to begin making comparisons between themselves and others. That is, their ideas about who they are come in part from how they are treated by others, as before, but increasingly they derive notions from *how they compare to their peers* (Harter, 1983; Ruble, Boggiano, Feldman, & Luebl, 1980). Studies of the social comparisons made by children show that even at the preschool age children are *aware* of how other children perform and how they are treated. It appears, however, that children's concerns at this young age have more to do with whether they are being treated fairly, relative to their peers, than with the implications of such differential treatment for their own self-concepts. Thus, differential treatment of siblings is likely to be seen by the five-year-old as unfairness on the part of a father, and by the eleven-year-old as unworthiness on the part of the child herself. Coming up short in comparison to others may have a different impact on the self-esteem of younger and older children. By the ages of nine or ten, children tend to evaluate themselves and their achievements by virtue of how they measure up to their peers.

The period of adolescence is seen by many as a particularly crucial time in the development of the self-concept: this is the time in which most individuals establish a self-identity that will persist into adult life. At about the age of 12 years—earlier in some cases and later in others—youngsters begin to display adult-like thinking styles. For the first time they are able to think abstractly, that is, imagine hypothetical possibilities, to introspect, or think about their own thoughts, and to think about how others see them (Flavell, 1985). These abilities allow for the development of three components of a mature self-concept, recognition of: (a) the *continuity* of the self over time; (b) the *unity* of the self in the face of different role and contextual demands; and (c) the *mutuality* of one's own and other's views of the self (Harter, 1983). As adolescents struggle to achieve a self-identity during the teenage years, they must come to resolve each of these issues.

Adolescents' new-found cognitive abilities, however, initially bring with them their own shortcomings. That is, young adolescents often become preoccupied with their new cognitive abilities in their search for a self-identity. The consequence may be that they become overly sensitive about how others see them, imagining, for instance, that they are more central in the thoughts of others than they really are. David Elkind (1978) has described this tendency as the young adolescent always feeling "on stage," playing before an "imaginary audience." The adolescent's recognition that he is unique may be seen in his construction of what Elkind calls a "personal fable"—an adolescent's idea that he has thoughts, feelings, motives, and experiences that others cannot comprehend, and, additionally, that he has a special destiny. Often an adolescent's belief in his own unique characteristics and special destiny are evaluated in a positive light—such as when a teenager believes that his parents cannot possibly understand and can never have experienced the quality of romantic love he feels for his girlfriend. Some young adolescents, however, may see their personal qualities or their destinies in a much more negative light. For instance, some adolescent suicides may stem, in part, from a teenager's idea that he is destined for a unique fate: that the world is watching him and will somehow be altered by his death. Practitioners need to understand these deep-seated and pervasive ideas of the developing adolescent, in terms of both their origins and their implications, if they are to intervene successfully in helping to foster positive and productive self-identities in young teens.

One further point that must be made, in regard to these age-related changes and their impact on self-concept, is that not all children develop all of the cognitive abilities that affect self-concept at the same rate. Thus, a child's ability to think abstractly may develop long before her disposition to use more differentiated concepts. Similarly, a youngster may acquire the ability to introspect before he has sufficient understanding of others to know how he differs from his peers. These dysynchronies, when children acquire related abilities at very different rates *or* when children are off-time relative to the development of their peers, may be an important source of self-concept problems.

Self-Control

Learning how to direct one's own behavior is a fundamental part of child development. In fact, most parents probably agree that one of their major concerns in child-rearing is to ensure that a child can regulate her *own* behavior. Parents want their children to be able to behave in acceptable ways when they themselves are absent, because part of grow-ing up means that children will spend increasing amounts of time on their own.

Self-control seems to be related to self-esteem in both direct and indirect ways (Harter, 1983). First, a child who is capable of directing her own activities and emotional expression may feel more *competent*. Second, a child who directs her behavior in socially acceptable and appro-priate ways is likely to receive more *approval* and positive regard from others. In fact, some studies have shown that children with high self-esteem also have stronger feelings of personal efficacy or feelings of con-trol (Harter, 1983). Additionally, styles of parental behavior that tend to best promote self-control in children, namely setting clear, consistent, and age-appropriate limits on child behavior and using reasoning (termed "authoritative parenting"), also tend to foster positive self-esteem in children (Maccoby & Martin, 1983).

The self-control process seems to involve three steps: (a) self-monitor-ing or being an observer of one's own actions; (b) self-evaluation, that is, knowing whether or not a given behavior is acceptable; and (3) self-reinforcement, or rewarding one's self for performing acceptable behaviors (Kanfer, 1970, 1971). Children at different ages will be more or less able to accomplish each of these tasks.

The development of self control in children goes through three major stages: control by caregivers; overt verbal control by the child; and covert control by the child. During infancy and early in the preschool years, children's behavior is controlled by the words and actions of others—such as their parents and caregivers. Adults control the young child's behavior *proactively* by arranging the physical environment (using gates for stairs, moving breakables) and establishing a satisfying routine (an early bedtime, a quiet time for an afternoon nap) so that the child is not given the opportunity to misbehave (such as by getting into forbidden activities or by being cranky or irritable). When adults control the young child's behavior *reactively*, they terminate misbehavior by their actions or words. In fostering self-control, spoken language is particularly import-ant because the child eventually must model such rules and strategies in controlling her own behavior. Thus, a firm "no-no," or "use your indoor voices," are statements that the young child can use on his own when adults are absent.

Early on, a child's own self-statements can actually interfere with the performance of a task. By the age of three or four, however, most children can use *spoken* language to guide their behavior. At younger ages children describe what they have done after completing a task; later they will use language in conjunction with their activities (as in play, when the child building with blocks mutters under her breath, ". . . this one goes here . . . . the red one goes here . . . . then put this on top. . . ."); only later will children actually use language to plan an activity *prior to* performing it. It is at this point that self-guiding functioning of language is established and takes its mature form, when spoken (overt) language "goes underground" as thought or covert speech.

During development the bases for self-control also seem to change. Harter (1983) describes the work of Loevinger (1976) who has identified a series of stages in self-control from infancy to adulthood. During the *impulsive stage* of infancy, actions are performed solely on the basis of whether they will be rewarded or punished, and rules are generally not understood. Later the child controls his behavior on the basis of *self-interest*. The third, *conformist* stage involves the child's following rules simply because they are rules. At this point he may be afraid to break rules because of disapproval from others. In the *conscientious* stage, the child's own conscience begins to operate, and we see the beginning of moral behavior; the child controls his misbehavior to avoid personal guilt rather than the condemnation of others. This period tends to last through the childhood years and into early adolescence. Some teens may move into the *autonomous* stage, during which the conflicting demands of personal and social needs and duties are recognized. At this time the young person realizes that expressing personal impulses may be acceptable when others are not hurt in the process. The highest, *integrated* stage, is rarely reached even by adults, and involves a reconciliation—not simply a recognition—of conflicts between personal needs and social demands.

The cognitive abilities underlying this developmental sequence are the same as those that influence the nature of the child's self-concept at different periods: from an orientation to the *concrete* and *immediate* (rewards and punishments or concept of the physical self) children develop *concepts* (moral rules or ideas about personal traits) which at first are *absolute* and *undifferentiated* (behaviors are right or wrong and personal characteristics are all or none). Only with the onset of adolescence does the youngster assume a more qualified and variegated view of himself and his behavior. It remains for the young adult to put the pieces together into an integrated whole.

As noted, the behavior of parents and other significant adults, together with her developing cognitive competencies, affect the child's ability to control her own actions. By placing sanctions on children's behavior, such as by using physical or psychological punishment (e.g., disapproval, rejection) the child seems to develop feelings of anxiety related to potential misbehaviors. This anxiety may later block the expression of inappropriate behaviors in the future. Verbal rationales which identify what behavior or activity is forbidden and why, and which provide appropriate alternative behaviors, also make punishment effective for inhibiting subsequent misbehavior (Parke, 1969).

Some recent evidence suggests that neither rewards (for good behavior) nor punishment should be extreme if attitudes about right and wrong are to be internalized by the child; that is, if they are to become part of the child's own value system. For instance, some studies have shown that while mild punishment makes activities less desirable, more severe punishment actually *increases* the attractiveness of a forbidden activity. Similarly, while small rewards may make an activity more desirable in future situations, large rewards make the same activity *less* attractive (Lepper, 1981). Thus, a child who is grounded for two weeks for playing in a vacant lot may come to think that this activity must be *extremely* desirable and is more likely to return to the play area than is a child who simply is told sternly that she has misbehaved. Similarly, a child who is paid ten dollars for an "A" on a test may come to think that studying *must* be very aversive (otherwise, why should she deserve such a reward?). Subsequently, she may be less likely to internalize a desire for academic achievement and less likely to direct her own behavior toward academic goals.

In addition to the child management strategies that adults apply, older preschoolers and school age children can be taught to control their behavior through private speech. Private speech is a term used to describe children's tendency to "talk to themselves" to guide their own behavior (Luria, 1961). Some research has shown that certain kinds of private speech tend to be more effective than others and that children of different ages respond better to certain kinds of self-instructions than to others. In helping children learn to resist temptation, for example, self-instructions that orient a child away from a tempting object or situation are most effective. A child may be taught how to *distract* herself ("go outside on the swings if you feel like taking a cookie"), or to *transform* a desired object into a neutral one ("imagine that the jellybeans are just buttons and the marshmallows are fluffy clouds") (Pressley, 1979). Other kinds of self statements, for instance those that focus on rewards ("if you don't *eat the candy* you'll lose weight) or that focus on a task rather than a tempting alternative ("think about what you have to do to *finish your homework*") are less effective than such temptation-inhibiting plans. Older children already may have an understanding about such plans and may use them spontaneously. As such, this kind of self-instructional training may be less successful for these youngsters.

Self-Esteem

We have noted the relationships between self-esteem and both self-concept and self-control: self-esteem has been defined as the discrepancy between one's actual self-concept and the ideal self; self-control has some bearing on whether children behave competently and appropriately and, in so doing, receive approval from others. We have seen that both children's self-concepts and their self-control abilities change with increasing maturity, and the nature of these changes must be kept in mind in our efforts to understand children's self-esteem and to design effective intervention strategies for promoting self-esteem in children of different ages.

Because both children's achievements (competencies) and the approval they receive from others provide the bases for their self-esteem, both of these dimensions are generally assessed in measures of self-esteem. Presumably, actual instrumental success *and* social approval give rise to the positive emotions associated with self-esteem (Harter, 1983).

One controversy having to do with the measurement of self-esteem is whether it is a unitary characteristic or whether self-esteem varies across different domains of activity (e.g., school performance versus peer popularity versus athletic ability). Some researchers in child development have argued that the young (preschool) child's cognitive level—in particular, the limitations in his conceptual abilities—make him unable to formulate an overall sense of self-esteem. On the other hand, neither can he make fine distinctions about his abilities in different areas of behavior. Rather, his "evaluations" of himself seem to arise in specific situations and are limited to those concrete experiences. In the case of elementary and junior high students, in contrast, a generalized self-evaluation is possible, but assessing self-esteem in specific domains also is important (Harter, 1983). In the late adolescent and early adult years, measuring *global* self-esteem may be more appropriate.

During childhood the specific domains relevant to children's feelings of self-worth change. Important dimensions for preschoolers include social approval, measured in terms of social acceptance by peers and mothers, and general competence, measured in terms of cognitive competence and physical abilities. In later childhood, however, this set of domains is modified to include athletic performance, academic achievement, appearance, conduct, peer acceptance, and general self-worth (Harter, 1983).

More detailed analyses have shown what it takes to make grade school children experience high self-esteem. In terms of general self-worth, for instance, positive self-esteem seems to be based on four factors (Harter, 1983): (a) children's relationships with their parents (whether they obey their parents; whether their parents show approval of them); (b) children's self-control of negative affect (whether they frequently lose their temper and get angry); (c) self-acceptance (the extent to which they are happy with themselves); and (d) social conduct (whether they get along with others; whether they do well in school). As children move into adolescence, we may find that social acceptance by peers becomes increasingly important for a youngster's general self-esteem. The extent to which the adolescent "fits in" to his world—family, peers, school, and possibly work—also helps to determine his self-esteem. As the adolescent struggles to form a unified self-identity, the consistency of demands from each of these different areas of his life may be particularly important to his feelings of self-esteem. The fact that this is a time when the youngster begins to participate in an increasingly wide variety of activities and to come into contact with a broader range of persons means that it may be more difficult to integrate and meet the often conflicting demands that the adolescent experiences.

SUMMARY

From the preschool years through adolescence, the ways children see themselves show dramatic changes. From ideas based on specific concrete experiences, children develop absolutist concepts of themselves that seem to be tied to different domains of experiences or ability and may be formed on the basis of feedback from others about what they are like. Later they begin to evaulate themselves on the basis of how their attributes or abilities compare to those of other youngers—for instance, siblings or peers. The onset of adolescence brings with it new cognitive skills which dispose the teenager to introspect, to possibly become preoccupied with how others see him, and to imagine what he can and might become in adult life. Simultaneously with these changes comes an increasing ability of the youngster to control her own behavior and thus, at least in part, to determine what kinds of reactions she receives from others (approval, disapproval) and in what areas she will excel.

Children change at different rates relative to their agemates; and furthermore, their abilities in some areas may develop more quickly or slowly than those in other areas. For instance, a very bright child who has advanced intellectual skills may have less social experience with peers and thereby be less competent at understanding the perspectives of others. Along these lines, a child who is competent in many areas (with peers, at school, in sports) may be experienced and proficient in directing her behavior toward positive goals, but may be less capable of self-control in situations of frustration resulting from failure. In both of these cases, children may be inclined to evaluate themselves negatively.

The sensitive practitioner must be able to recognize a child's level of abilities in the areas of social, cognitive, and emotional functioning in order to understand how that child sees himself and why. Not only will a child's developmental level(s) affect the goals and areas of functioning chosen for intervention, but, as we suggest in the following section, assessment and treatment procedures may need to be modified as well.

Developmental Considerations in Assessment and Treatment Procedures

In early sessions with a teacher or counselor, children may display a great deal of variability in their understanding of and reaction to the intervention program. The increased self-consciousness of some preadolescents and adolescents may mean that being targeted for special treatment only increases their self-doubts. Thus, extra care should be given to explain the rationale for and purposes behind the intervention. Older youngsters may be particularly concerned about the confidentiality of the information they provide, both during the initial assessment and during discussion in later sessions. Given their increased preoccupation with the image they present to peers, parents, and significant adults in their lives, it will be important for the counselor to talk to these youngsters about who will have access to material from the assessment and treatment sessions.

In addition, on account of their more mature status, older children may want to and be more able to provide input regarding the direction of treatment. One important difference in the kinds of treatment children receive in the program described in this book is the difference between altering children's standards (or ideas about their "ideal" selves) and altering their behavior (or their "real" selves). An older youngster may be in a better position to decide whether he wants to learn to behave in ways that are valued by his peers (in an effort to become popular) or, instead, to alter his standards about what is important to him (for instance, to excel in academics even though others think he is a "nerd"). Finally, in working with children it is always important to remember that they frequently have not chosen to come for treatment. For this reason, practitioners who work with children need to maintain an upbeat and encouraging attitude and to plan sessions that are fun and interesting for their clients.

Both the initial "getting acquainted" period and the way in which the assessments are conducted will vary, depending upon a child's developmental status. Whereas more mature youngsters will be able to carry on a conversation with the counselor, rapport may be better established with younger children via a game. In fact, for the most part, younger children will require more concrete exercises, for instance with props such as pictures or puppets, whereas in the case of older youngsters, words will suffice. Similarly, with younger children verbal responses may be fairly limited. For this reason you may need to provide choices (such as pictures) for the child to use in describing her thoughts or feelings. Similarly, rather than requiring verbal responses to open-ended questions, you can give the child a choice of two or more alternatives that you verbalize (for instance, "Do you usually feel like you're a pretty friendly person or do you usually feel like a pretty unfriendly person?").

If standardized questionnaires are being used, items will need to be read to the less advanced child and allowances made for her smaller vocabulary and more limited comprehension. Older children may be able to fill out questionnaires independently, and, given their increased self-consciousness, they may prefer this more "private" mode of describing themselves. Some youngsters, due to their learning problems, may experience a great deal of frustration in reading through a questionnaire—which, in turn, may be reflected in how they respond to the items. It is important that the counselor prepare for such a possibility by examining the youngster's educational record or talking to his teachers. A special "answer sheet" may be prepared in advance for such a child so that the counselor can read the items on a questionnaire and the youngster can respond in private.

One difficulty with using standardized tests of "personality"—those measuring characteristics or "traits"—with younger children is that the answers they give will be less consistent over time. That is, because the younger child's ideas about herself are tied to specific experiences, they may change from day to day. Not until later, during the school age years, do youngsters seem to establish relatively stable ideas about themselves and others. Additionally, whereas many adolescents will have spent some time thinking about who they are and about their relationships with others, school age children (e.g., those from 7–12 years) may have more difficulty in answering questions about themselves, at least initially, because they have not yet developed an introspective style of thought.

These developmental differences have implications for other forms of assessment as well. For instance, when the counselor obtains information about a child's behavior, either through direct observation or reports from significant adults, a child's developmental level may have an effect on: (a) how emotional distress such as that stemming from low self-esteem will be expressed, and (b) the pervasiveness of self-esteem problems. The younger child is likely to express his distress in concrete, acting out behavior. For older youngsters, in contrast, distress may be turned inward and may be observed as moodiness, sadness, or withdrawal. The younger child's problem also may be limited to specific situations. On the other hand, because she has a more stable and generalized self-concept, the older youngster's problems may be evident across a variety of contexts (at home and school, with peers and adults).

Along these lines, youngsters with more advanced cognitive skills may be better able to generalize what they learn in treatment sessions to new situations and to describe to the counselor, instances in which general kinds of problems or concerns arise. The less sophisticated child, however, may need a broader range of concrete examples and more elaborated practice (for instance, role playing) in handling the range of problem situations.

In terms of structure, sessions for older youngsters can last longer (approximately one hour) and can be conducted on a weekly basis. Given the younger child's shorter attention span and different sense of time, half hour sessions twice a week may be more effective. Along these lines, older youngsters may be able to undertake more elaborated homework or independent practice sessions. In contrast, children in the primary school grades will be less likely to complete such assignments or may need help and support in doing so from parents or teachers.

CONCLUSIONS

As we have seen, individual differences between children in terms of their behavioral, cognitive, biological, and emotional development will influence the effectiveness of treatment goals and strategies. In concluding this chapter, we would like to raise two additional points for the reader's consideration.

First, although we have described variations in strategies and goals mostly in terms of younger versus older children, the practitioner must remember that age is only a rough index of children's developmental status. Children of the same chronological age may be very different in terms of their maturity; moreover, a given child may be at different levels in different domains of functioning (cognitive, behavioral, emotional, physical).

A second issue is that developmental status is not the only characteristic with an important impact on the effectiveness of a given treatment: other factors, such as a child's gender, whether she has a learning problem or is intellectually gifted, the nature of her family background—such as her race, social class or even her position in the constellation of siblings—may all determine what the appropriate goals and strategies of intervention might be. In intervening to foster a child's self-esteem it will be important, for instance, to know the extent to which a child's characteristics match the standards set by her social environment. For instance, low self-esteem in a minority child living in an white upper middle-class environment may be altogether a different phenomenon (and consequently, require different goals and strategies for intervention) than low self-esteem exhibited by a child whose family background matches that of her peers.

Chapter 4

How to Use This Manual

The process of enhancing self-esteem can be broadly categorized into assessment and intervention. By assessment we refer to the process of determining the specific strengths and weaknesses of a child in the various domains of self-esteem. Intervention is the process by which change is actually accomplished. This chapter describes the way in which this manual can be employed in assessment and intervention in the process of enhancing self-esteem.

ASSESSMENT

Assessment of children with low self-esteem is a difficult matter, since low self-esteem is often accompanied by other problems. Children who are withdrawn, hyperactive, aggressive, or below average academically may all have problems with self-esteem, yet they are very different in other ways. The choice of whether to treat first the low self-esteem or the other problems is left to the practitioner, with one suggestion: children with difficulties such as impulsivity or hyperactivity should be treated for these behavior problems first, if they are severe enough to interfere with the ability to benefit from a structured program such as this. Of course, it is always possible that behavior problems are a symptomatic expression of low self-esteem, and that treating the underlying self-esteem problem may result in changes across several domains, including behavior.

Discovering the innermost thoughts and feelings of a child is always problematic. For this reason, a broad assessment is recommended. The goal is to gather information from various sources: the child's self-report, parent and teacher interviews, behavioral observations, and paper-and-pencil measures. No one source can be considered to be entirely accurate; instead, collect information in several places and look for similar patterns to emerge. A clear conception of the child's particular pattern of strengths and weaknesses will enable you to be of greater help to him.

In more specific terms, what you will be searching for are two main areas of information.

1. The child's capabilities—what he's good at, what he enjoys, what he cannot do as well
2. The child's feelings and thoughts about his capabilities—what he's proud and ashamed of, what ways he would like to be different, his ideals and goals.

Keep in mind the five components of self-esteem described in chapter 1—social, academic, family, body, and global. You need to know about the child's behavioral, cognitive, emotional, and biological development in each of these areas.

Parent Interview

It is often helpful to meet with the parents before interviewing the child, since the material gained from them can give you more direction when you do the child interview. Much of what you should try to obtain from the parents is straightforward information—their views of the child's abilities, interests, and goals, as well as how they think he feels about these areas. Remember that parental input must be treated as a "working hypothesis" in your information-gathering process, not as absolute truth.

In addition, be alert to "between the lines" information that parents give you. You need to obtain a sense of their attitudes toward the child and his strengths and weaknesses. Are the parents supportive, overprotective, critical, blaming? Do they make excuses for him? Are their expectations reasonable? You can be sure that the parents' style of approaching the child's areas of ability and inability will be mirrored somewhere in the child's own views of himself, both in his family self-esteem and in other areas. This material is often more easily (and honestly) obtained through observation of subtleties than by direct questioning.

Child Interview

Your meeting with the child is probably the most important part of the assessment, and perhaps the most complicated as well. In your approach, you will need to create a careful balance between structure and openness. It is essential that you structure this interview so you can gather the information you need, yet it must be done in an open manner so that the child feels comfortable about conveying her thoughts and feelings to you. In addition, the child's age and level of cognitive sophistication will affect the techniques you use to learn about her (Bierman, 1983).

Begin the interview with a brief statement about the reason for the interview—something like "This will give us a chance to get to know each other. I'd like to learn about the things you like and dislike. And sometimes kids find that there are some things I can do to help things go better for them." The first task is to get comfortable with each other. A younger child (age 8–10) may want to explore the playroom or play a game with you. Older children who are more verbally inclined can participate in casual conversation with you. Keep the tone light and non-threatening at first.

After a few minutes you can try shifting the focus to the child's interests. It may be less threatening to make a list of "Likes" and "Dislikes" rather than using a standard interview format. Younger children may enjoy drawing happy, sad, mad, and scared faces at the top of a page so that you can list the things that make them feel that way under each face. School age children, who are accustomed to a task orientation, respond well to creating lists: "I need to list three things that make you feel good (bad) when you're with your friends (or with family, or at school, etc.)." This approach takes the pressure off the child, since attention is placed on completing the list. More discussion can be elicited with the use of structured probes: "How often does that happen?" "What is it about recess that makes you happy?" "What do the kids at school tease you about?" Adolescents, who are notorious for being close-mouthed, generally are more communicative with structured questions than with open-ended ones ("Tell me about your friends" is likely to meet with an answer like "They're OK."). Your tone should be friendly and matter of fact; excessive warmth and empathy can overwhelm children at any of these ages.

You may want to follow up on any leads you obtained in the first part of the interview or from the parent interview. Elaborations can sometimes be elicited through story completions ("I knew a boy your age whose parents argued a lot. What do you think they fought about? How did it make the boy feel?") or sentence completion ("I hate it when ___" or "I feel best when ___" or "The thing I'd like most to change about myself is ___"). Younger children may enjoy using dolls, puppets, or pictures to finish the stories. Having clay or Lego blocks available to occupy an older child's hands while she's talking can create a more comfortable atmosphere. Adolescents may find it easier to talk if you create a more informal atmosphere, by taking a walk, for example.

Of course, children will not always tell you what you want to know. Refusal to discuss a topic should be respected, but is valuable information in itself; it may very well indicate an area of difficulty.

Much can be learned by observing a child's behavior and emotional tone during the interview. Agitation or anxiety can indicate a problem with the current topic of discussion. Also, the child's response to you can be indicative of her feelings of confidence in this unusual situation. Does she wait for your direction or plunge enthusiastically into an activity? Does she cling to you for reassurance? Does she brag and show off? The behaviors you see in the interview should not be assumed to be typical for her in all situations, but they can provide you with some clues.

Leave some time at the end of the session for a pleasant activity you can do together—a game for a younger child, a switch to more nonthreatening topics for an adolescent. It is best for her to leave feeling relaxed and positive about the time she has spent with you.

Teacher Interview

Teachers have a unique perspective on a child; school is the arena in which many of children's mastery experiences occur, and so teachers have an excellent opportunity to observe a child's dealings with success and failure. Also, with the hectic schedules of families, children sometimes spend more time during the day with their teachers than with their parents.

Teachers tend to be very busy, but even 15 minutes can yield valuable information if you ask the right questions. Again, you will be trying to learn about the child's competencies and his feelings about the things he can and cannot do. You might begin by asking the teacher to describe the strengths and weaknesses of the child in the areas of academics, interpersonal (social) skills, and individual qualities. This should give you plenty of information to pursue further. Some things you may want to be looking for:

Is the child generally successful or unsuccessful in his attempts?

How does he respond to success and failure?

Does he set goals that are too easy or too hard?

Does he approach new situations with confidence or trepidation?

Does the child appear to be satisfied with his academic achievement? With his friendships?

Is he well accepted by same-sex classmates? (For adolescents, information about opposite-sex peers is relevant also.)

Observations

Observing a child in his natural surroundings is an excellent way of learning about his capabilities. This is especially valuable for analyzing his social skills. Perhaps the best settings for this type of observation are the school playground during recess or the cafeteria at lunchtime. Ideally, you should be able to get close enough to hear the interactions that occur but without being intrusive. (Adolescents will typically be much more reactive to an observer than younger children, even to the point of making it impossible for you to observe.) Watch the child's ability to enter and leave a group. Does he become part of the group smoothly? Do the others welcome him, or protest? Does he seem to be fully a part of the group, or does he hover around the edges watching? When he leaves the group, does he speak to the other children, or does he drift away unnoticed? Notice his abilities in resolution of problems. Can he work out a disagreement without resorting to physical or verbal aggression? Can he resume the interaction after the conflict is resolved? Pay attention to the attitudes of the other children toward him. Do they seek him out or avoid him? Do they bully him or tease him? Keep in mind, of course, that what you observe may be significantly better or worse than his typical behavior. It's usually a good idea to ask the child's teacher how your observations correspond to his usual performance.

Tests

Tests are generally of limited usefulness for this specific assessment of self-esteem, but they can add some information to what you gather from interviews and observations. Tests are a quick and easy means of obtaining information, and children may be more honest on paper than face to face; however, these answers lack the richness gained from interviews. Three tests to consider are described here.

The Piers–Harris Children's Self-Concept Scale (Piers, 1976) is frequently used. It has the advantage of being well normed, so a child can be easily compared to his peers. This test will result in one score, intended to be used as an indicator of global self-esteem. It will probably add little to a complete assessment other than a type of documentation of the child's status in regard to self-image. The Piers-Harris could, however, be useful as a screening device.

The Harter Perceived Competence Scale (Harter, 1985) is more likely to increase your knowledge about the child. It is composed of four subscales: global, social, academic, and physical. This is a measure of self-*concept*, though—items reflect the child's assessment of his competencies (for example, number of friends, abilities at sports and games) rather than his feelings about himself. Still, this can be valuable information as long as you avoid confusing it with self-esteem. A nice feature is a companion test for the child's teacher to complete; this test is considered by Harter to be a more objective view of the child's abilities.

An unpublished test developed by Alice Pope, the Five-Scale Test of Self-Esteem for Children, is included in the appendix of this book along with scoring instructions. Due to the lack of psychometric data on this test, it cannot be used as a standardized test, but the results can be helpful as part of a clinical assessment. The Five-Scale Test is composed of subscales which measure five components of self-esteem: global, academic, social, body, and family. This test can be useful for comparing the relative strengths and weaknesses of the five components, and for using the responses to individual items to help create a descriptive picture of the child.

Putting It All Together

If you have followed the assessment plan outlined in this chapter, you now have a wealth of information about the child. Making sense out of it can be a major task. To help put it in order, use the checklist provided in the appendix. The checklist is not exhaustive, but may be useful in helping you to organize the data you have collected. When you've finished checking off all the items, look to see whether the preponderance of checks is in the positive or negative self-esteem column. Naturally, this is more complex than simply counting check marks and coming to a "majority wins" type of conclusion. You may notice that the child has more difficulty with some components of self-esteem than others; in fact, he may have serious difficulties in one area but be fine in another. This sort of pattern, where there is a mixture of highs and lows, is not uncommon.

If the child has one or more areas of low self-esteem, you may want to consider using the treatment plan outlined in this book. A few recommendations:

First, in order for a child to benefit from this program she must be sufficiently advanced in her cognitive development that she can begin to work with abstractions, such as thinking about her own thoughts and feelings. We feel that most children are unable to do this until they reach third grade. There is a lot of individual variability, however, so age cannot be used as the only determinant. If you are unsure about a child's cognitive ability, try a session or two of the program and see how she does. A careful reading of chapter 3 will be helpful in evaluating the child's readiness.

Second, you must be willing to work through the entire program. Your treatment will be ineffective if you choose pieces here and there from the program, since it was designed to be a coherent whole, with each session building on the previous ones.

Third, a child with serious behavior problems—ones which would interfere with her ability to sit quietly and concentrate for 30 minutes—will not be able to benefit from this program until her behavior is under control.

And last, a child need not have major difficulties with self-esteem for her to benefit from this program. Because the program teaches skills which can be used throughout the child's life, it can be seen as a preventive effort which might forestall more serious problems in the future. Most children (and many adults!) could profit from using these healthier approaches in their lives.

USING THE TREATMENT SESSIONS

If you have followed the assessment procedures outlined above, you should already be well acquainted with the child and have established a good rapport. Your role now will be that of a teacher who is accepting and warm—your job is to instruct the child in new skills, within an atmosphere of caring and trust. Begin the first session by explaining the purpose of the treatment: to teach him some new ways to handle problems that come up in his life, so that he will feel good about himself. It is very important that you constantly convey to the child your faith in his ability to master these new skills.

It is recommended that the program be scheduled into 30 to 60 minute sessions once or twice weekly; less frequent meetings may dilute the effectiveness of the program, especially for younger children. As mentioned in chapter 3, half-hour sessions twice a week may be more effective for younger children, while adolescents might do well with weekly hour-long sessions.

The program has been designed to build upon itself, session by session. Be sure that each skill has been mastered before moving on. There is nothing sacred about the number of sessions used, as long as all the material is covered in order. Children will vary in the length of time and practice needed to master a skill, so be prepared to be flexible in this respect. For some children, the cognitive skills are intuitively obvious, and they require only the briefest discussion (however, be sure to have them do the homework so you know they can use the skills in practice). Other children are bewildered by some of the topics—be patient and take the time to explain and give examples over and over, even if you need to spend 3 or 4 sessions on the same topic. You may have to review a particular skill, such as problem solving, when it comes up in a later session. The key is to to whatever is necessary to assure that the child understands *and* is able to use the group of skills taught in the program.

The homework assignments are a critical part of the program. Intelligent children can often display an impressive intellectual understanding of a skill, but may be utterly at a loss when asked to put it into practice. If you want children to be able to use these skills in their lives, you have to encourage them to practice in real situations. Homework should be assigned at the end of every session, and be the first thing discussed at the start of the following session. Avoid punitive responses when a child neglects to do her homework, but be firm—explain that doing the homework is the *only* way to really learn the skills. Back-up reinforcement may be necessary if the child continues to resist (see chapter 13, Special Issues).

Although the program is a structured one, there is room for tailoring your procedures to the individual. In fact, the success of your efforts will be greatly enhanced if you do so. Children's responses to the program will vary according to their age, areas of interest and competence, type of difficulties with self-esteem, and their goals for themselves. Each of these factors should be considered by the practitioner.

Age

The program usually works best with children at about third grade and older. As written, the material is geared for pre-adolescents. In general, younger children (below 10–12) will need more concrete examples, due to their level of cognitive functioning. Most adolescents can benefit from the program as it is presented, but examples more applicable to their interests and needs should be substituted when necessary. Suggestions for adapting the sessions to younger children and adolescents are included in the treatment chapters; it will also be helpful to consult chapter 3 when attempting to design the treatment for the proper developmental level of the child.

Areas of Interest and Competence

It is always important to build on a child's strengths. Examples should always be as closely related to his life as possible. In the standard setting and attributional style sections, for example, be sure that you and the child are talking about situations that pertain to her interests—how does she feel when she makes a mistake during a music lesson or when she wins a tennis match? Knowing the child's skills is also important because you need to help her feel good about those abilities. Children with low self-esteem sometimes discount their strengths as unimportant; instead, they need to learn to derive satisfaction from them.

Types of Difficulties with Self-Esteem

As described in the section on assessment in this chapter and in chapter 1, children's self-esteem centers around the areas of family relationships, social interactions, academic success, body image, and a global self-evaluation. The importance of these areas varies due to individual and developmental differences, as described in chapter 3. It is important to have an idea about which areas are problematic for the child. Areas in which he has a positive self image can be emphasized in order to point out their value to the child. Areas of difficulty should become direct targets of the intervention.

Goals

A child whose experiences seldom match up to his goals will have low self-esteem. His goals may not always be appropriate for him, however. One 11-year-old girl felt dissatisfied with her social relationships because she wanted to be a member of the "popular" group in her class. This group was composed of 12-year-old girls whose main interests were hairstyles, designer jeans, and boys. The younger girl did not share their interests; she enjoyed writing, playing the piano, reading, and computer puzzles. Still, she aspired to be one of them. Finally she said, "You know, if I was friends with them, I'd have to do the things they're interested in. I think I'd rather have one or two close friends who like the same things I do." If a child's goals are, in your opinion, reasonable and attainable for her, your job will be helping her develop the necessary skills. If not, you will have to guide her in adjusting her goals. Bear in mind, however, that this decision is ultimately her own—you cannot impose your values on her. The material on standard setting (chapter 9) may be helpful to the child when making these decisions.

Special Problems

Sometimes problems arise in spite of your best efforts. If things are not going well, reread this chapter (particularly the end of the Assessment section, which describes the type of child best suited for this program, and the entire section on Using the Treatment Sessions) and consult chapter 13.

Chapter 5

Social Problem Solving

Each one of us is constantly facing problems and deciding how to handle them. Many times, the process of solving everyday problems is so automatic that we are unaware of exactly how we do it. Nonetheless, it must be recognized that without the ability to identify difficulties and arrive at workable solutions, our daily lives would be paralyzed.

Children, too, face problems every day. They encounter teasing from classmates and anxiety about tests or being left out of games or other activities. Often, adults are available to help. However, children can solve many of their own problems without adult assistance. Even young children can learn the steps involved in effective problem solving.

There are a number of advantages for children who acquire the skill of problem solving. Children who have been taught to use systematic problem-solving strategies tend to cope more effectively with stress and frustration. Competence with problem solving also seems to have a positive impact on academic performance. Further, research has shown that children and adolescents with strong skills in this area are less likely to become delinquent, to abuse drugs and alcohol, or to develop serious psychological problems. At a most basic level, the ability to solve problems autonomously can be a source of pride and positive self-esteem for a child.

In this chapter, we present the problem-solving model, along with an example of how it is used and a discussion of developing cognitive and social abilities and their relationship to problem solving. We also provide strategies for assessment and intervention. As was mentioned in chapter 2, a problem-solving approach can be taken with difficulties in everyday life, as well as with the process of enhancing self-esteem.

Problem-Solving Model

The affective, cognitive, and behavioral domains are involved in problem solving. Emotions are often the first clue that a problem exists and must be solved. Cognitions are used in identification of the problem, strategizing about possible solutions and their consequences, and making a plan to carry out the best solution. Finally, behavioral skills must be used to complete the sequence. Although the process is somewhat complex, it can be taught successfully when the process is broken down into several steps. D'Zurilla and Goldfried (1971) developed this type of step-by-step model for teaching problem solving; presented here is our adaptation of that model.

1. The first step is to recognize that a problem exists. This involves monitoring one's own feelings in order to detect anger, worry, sadness, or other discomfort. Negative feelings are the cue to begin problem solving.
2. As soon as a problem is detected, stop and think. Just for a moment, step aside from the situation (either physically or mentally) and decide what the problem is.
3. Once the problem is clearly identified, it is time to decide on a goal. What is the desired outcome for the situation?
4. Now, think of many different possible solutions. At this point, don't evaluate; just generate possibilities, no matter how far-fetched. Be creative.
5. Next, think about the consequences that are likely to result from each of these solutions.
6. By now, some solutions will appear to be better than others. Choose a solution or combination of solutions, based on the ease or difficulty of carrying it out and the desirability of the consequences.
7. Finally, make a plan for implementing the chosen solution. Each step should be thought out before acting.

To clarify the use of the problem-solving model, we will elaborate with an example. A child named Andrea is involved in an activity with a group of her friends. All are enjoying themselves until another girl, Janey, approaches the group, asking to join in the game. Janey is not well liked by her classmates; she is different in the way she dresses and behaves, and the other children think she is peculiar. Some of the children in the group begin to tease her, calling her names and saying they will not allow her to play with them. Andrea does not particularly like Janey but feels uncomfortable that her friends are being mean to her.

1. *Realize that there is a problem.* Andrea's feelings of discomfort—probably her empathy with Janey's embarrassment—are a cue to her that she has a problem to solve.
2. *Stop and think. Decide what the problem is.* Andrea should take no further action until she identifies the problem and decides what to do. After thinking about the situation, she decides the problem is that she thinks it is wrong to make fun of other people.
3. *Decide on a goal.* Andrea would like the others to stop teasing Janey.
4. *Think of possible solutions.*
   (a) Andrea could tell the other children to stop teasing Janey.
   (b) Andrea and Janey could go play by themselves.
   (c) Andrea could get mad at the others and tell them they are mean and stupid for teasing Janey.
   (d) Andrea could tell the teacher.
5. *Think about the consequences for each solution.*
   (a) The other children might listen to Andrea. Or they might ignore her, and could start teasing Andrea, too.
   (b) The other children would probably stop teasing Janey, but they might not want to be friends with Andrea.
   (c) The other children might get mad at Andrea. They might or might not stop teasing Janey.
   (d) The teacher could tell them to stop bothering Janey. The other children might think Andrea was a tattle-tale.
6. *Choose the best solution.* Andrea decides that her first idea, to talk to the others, will work best to accomplish her goal.
7. *Make a plan for carrying out the solution.* Andrea knows that the way she talks with the others will affect their response. She decides to try to direct their attention away from Janey and back onto the game by saying something like, "Oh come on, it's more fun to play." If they do not listen right away, she will encourage one or two of the girls to start playing the game and hope the others will follow.

As you can see from this example, seldom are there clear-cut right and wrong solutions; the individual must make a judgment about the best solution, based on the predicted outcomes. The way in which a solution is carried out can be crucial to its success (it is at this point that social skills are most necessary). With experience and instruction, children can greatly improve their ability to generate and choose good solutions and to implement them skillfully.

THE DEVELOPMENT OF
PROBLEM-SOLVING SKILLS

Age differences will also affect a child's ability to acquire and use social problem-solving skills. Younger school-age children tend to be concrete in their thinking, so it will be important to use specific examples and to relate them carefully to each of the problem-solving steps. Some children may have difficulty with causal reasoning, logic, sequential thinking, and/or memory abilities, all of which are required in problem-solving planning. In order to train problem-solving skills, it will be necessary to determine whether a child's limitations fall in any of these areas.

An additional problem young children may have is that they tend to have fairly rigid thoughts about right and wrong, and they may rely more on adults to determine the "right" answer. These children will benefit from a greater degree of adult structuring (e.g., helping the child to evaluate the advantages and disadvantages of the solutions he has generated) and support of his ability to think for himself.

Upper elementary-age children generally enjoy training in problem solving. They have a clear understanding of rule-based activities, and find it easy to relate this ability to the problem-solving steps. The capacity to solve their own problems autonomously is very consistent with their desire to be more independent of parents and teachers. These children also have a clear need for this skill, as they begin to encounter more situations where they are expected to function without constant adult supervision.

Most adolescents have rapidly-developing abilities in abstract thinking, and they should be able to use the problem-solving steps without difficulty. They have the potential to become quite sophisticated in evaluating the relative benefits of various solutions. For teenagers, there are conflicting pressures to conform to the values of the family and the peer group, and consequently they may need support in acting in accordance with their own beliefs.

In addition to cognitive development, the developmental level of social skills will have an impact upon the success of a child's efforts to problem solve. Cognitive skills are sufficient to create a well thought-out plan; however, the plan must be carried out, and it is this behavioral component that can sometimes be troublesome for a child. For this reason, it is critical that the child practice using the problem-solving steps outside of the training sessions. Chapter 11 addresses the training of communication skills, which are often necessary to implement the solution to a problem.

ASSESSING CHILDREN'S
PROBLEM SOLVING

Adolescent Self and Context Measure
(Elias, 1981)

Read these items to the child and record her responses. Evaluate her natural use of any of the problem-solving steps. Make note of weak areas in order to focus on these during the intervention phase. Specifically, evaluate the child's ability to anticipate realistic consequences (as in part *a* of each problem). Planning is assessed in part *b*. Finally, responses to obstacles which arise in trying a solution are elicited in parts *c* and *d*.

Problem #1

A group of kids in your class are getting together to make a team. You would like to join, but they do not ask you. You are upset about this, and you want to join the team.

a. Let's say you think about getting even with the other kids for leaving you out. Try to name five different things that might happen if you try to get even.

b. Let's say you think about the problem and decide your best solution is to ask to join the team. What do you need to think about so that your solution will work?

c. Let's say you ask the other kids if you can join the team. What if they say they're sorry, but they have no more room on the team. What might happen next?

d. Let's say you ask the other kids if you can join, and they say, "No, we don't want you." What might happen next?

Problem #2

You are in class, having a math lesson. The teacher reads from the book and calls on you to answer. You answer, but you are wrong. A few other kids laugh at you. You are upset at this, and you do not want to be laughed at again.

a. Let's say you think about yelling at the other kids. Try to name five things that might happen if you yell at them.

b. Let's say you think about the problem and decide your best solution is to ask the other kids not to laugh at you. What do you need to think about so that your solution will work?

c. Let's say you ask the other kids not to laugh at you, but at recess they start laughing at you again. What might happen next?

d. Let's say you ask the other kids to not laugh at you, and they won't talk to you any more, and they are going to tell other kids not to be your friend. What might happen next?

Self-Report

A practical way to evaluate the use of good problem solving is to simply talk with the child. Ask him for an example of a recent problem he solved well, and another he felt he did not handle well. Listen to his description of the problem situation and find out what his thoughts were in making a decision. Make note of solutions which rely on aggression, pestering, wishful thinking (where the problem is magically solved without any efforts by the child to accomplish this), or giving up. More positive are solutions involving compromise and cooperation, discussion, asking for help from peers or adults, and avoidance of aggression. Next, ask questions about each of the problem-solving steps. For example, ask how he knew the situation was a problem. What feeling did he have? Did he make a clear identification of the problem for himself? Then ask if he considered more than one solution. What were they? Did he think about what might happen if he tried those solutions? Did he have a goal he was aiming for? How did he decide what to do? Did he make a plan before he acted? Children who are unaccustomed to a reflective style of thinking will have difficulty understanding some of these questions, and they will need additional practice to acquire problem-solving skills. Children who are ready to begin learning problem solving will be able to think about many of the questions, even if they did not use some of the steps. Even children who appear to be making sensible decisions can benefit from training in problem solving; knowing and using a systematic approach to solving problems can be a preventative approach to coping with life's stressors and problems.

INTERVENTIONS

Problem-Solving Orientation

Introduce the child to a "problem-solving orientation." The following points should be explained and discussed.

1. Problems are a normal part of daily life.
2. Children can solve many of their own problems without enlisting the help of adults. (Help the child give some examples of problems which she could solve by herself.)
3. Feelings are important cues to the existence of a problem. (Give some examples, such as angry feelings which result from a disagreement

with a friend, or scared feelings which arise when you realize you've gotten lost on a hike.)
4. When you realize you have a problem, the first thing to do is "stop and think"—that is, don't do anything more until you've carefully thought out the next step.

Basic Feeling Identification

Before he can learn the problem-solving steps, the child may need some work in identifying his feelings, so that he can recognize problems when they occur. Begin by explaining that feelings are part of everyday living and that they can be very useful to us in helping us to understand ourselves better. Have the child list as many feelings as he can think of for a few minutes. Explain that some basic feelings are; happy, sad, scared, and angry. There are many names for feelings that describe different types of happiness, sadness, fear, and anger, but these are some basic feelings. For each feeling, have the child make a list of things that make him feel that way. Write down his lists. Next, ask him how he knows he is experiencing these feelings. He will probably have difficulty answering this question, so explain that feelings have physiological (body) cues associated with them. For example, sadness might be felt as a heaviness or sinking feeling in the stomach, along with a feeling of droopiness in the facial muscles. There might also be tears or a lump in the throat. Happiness, for some people, is felt by a lightness in the stomach or chest area and a lifting of the facial muscles into a smile. Anger is often expressed in the body by muscle tension in the face (especially the jaw), neck, shoulders, and torso. Some children mention a feeling of "burning" or "like I'm about to explode" inside them when they are angry. Being scared may be accompanied by a number of physical cues, such as sweaty palms, faster breathing and heartbeat, a type of muscle tension that is a feeling of "jumpiness," widened eyes, and "fluttery" feelings in the stomach. Allow the child to describe his own sensations before telling him the ones listed here; use these to help him think of more complete descriptions of his own responses. In order for younger children to do this, you may have to help them imagine situations which induce these feeling states. It is important to stress that individuals differ in their responses, and that it is better for him to discover his own individual responses than to think about matching some "standard" response.

Problem-Solving Steps

Now, the child should be ready to learn the steps of problem solving.

1. Realize that there is a problem.
2. Stop and think. Decide what the problem is.
3. Decide on a goal (what you want to happen).
4. Think of many possible solutions.
5. Think about the consequences for each solution (what would happen if you tried it).
6. Choose the best solution.
7. Make a step-by-step plan for carrying out the solution.

List the steps on a blackboard or piece of paper so the child can see them. Younger children may need to use simplified language, perhaps the rewording enclosed in parenthesis for steps 3 and 5. Explain what is involved in each step (as we did earlier in this chapter).

Once the child understands the problem-solving steps, ask her for a problem that she has encountered and use it as an example for going through all seven steps. Write the problem, solutions, and consequences on a blackboard or paper as you discuss each step. If the child cannot think of a personal example, suggest a situation; for example, getting lost in a new school, having a problem with a teacher (have the child help you specify the problem), or making new friends. It is helpful to repeat this exercise two or three times with different problems.

Younger children will have a harder time remembering the steps, and they will need more concrete examples. For all ages, it is imperative that they practice this skill outside of treatment sessions (see homework section at the end of this chapter).

Adolescent Self and Context Exercises

For additional practice, use as exercises the two problems in the Adolescent Self and Context Measure (Elias, 1981), which was used in the assessment phase. Now that the child has had some instruction in problem solving, have her evaluate her original responses. Discuss with her the pros and cons involved in different choices.

Problem Situations—Elementary Age Children

The situations presented here are opportunities for the child to practice applying the problem-solving steps to sample problems. If children are initially unable to use all seven problem solving steps due to the inability to remember and manipulate so much material, simplify the process into four steps:

1. What is the problem?
2. What are some solutions?
3. What would happen if I tried these solutions?
4. Which is the best solution?

It may be helpful for you to record the child's thoughts and act as "memory" for her by keeping track of proposed solutions, etc. Once the child masters four steps, expand to the full seven-step model. Provide guidance as necessary to keep the child realistic and sensible about problem identification, goals, consequences, and optimal solutions. Also, if she misses an obvious solution or consequence, you may want to suggest it. From time to time, introduce an obstacle to her chosen solution, and help her to problem solve ways to overcome the new problem. For example, in the second practice situation below, the child might decide to make an agreement with the younger sibling to not follow her around any more. Accept this solution, and then ask what she would do if the sibling broke the agreement and started following her again.

In addition to the situations supplied here, you and/or the child can create your own.

1. You have asked your parents for a pet, and they have suggested a goldfish. What you would really like is a cat or dog, but your parents think that would be too much work and responsibility.
2. Your younger sister/brother wants to follow you everywhere and do everything you do. You complain to your parents but they say, "Be nice to him/her."
3. Your brother/sister always starts fights with you, and then you both get in trouble. You're tired of your parents being mad at you for something you didn't start.
4. Sometimes when you go over to your friend's house to play, he/she has another person over and they won't let you play. You feel left out.
5. You would like to wear more stylish clothes, like your friends, but your parents won't let you.
6. You tried out for a sports team but didn't make it. Now all your friends are always at practice and you have nobody to play with.
7. You and your best friend get along really well except for one thing— he/she always cheats at games, but will never admit it.
8. Your parents told you never to leave your bike outside overnight, but you did anyway. This morning your bike was gone.

9. You have a big test coming up, and you're really worried about it. You're afraid you'll never be able to pass it.
10. Your friend has started to hang around with other kids and won't talk to you anymore. You don't know why, and you feel left out.
11. You and your friends would like to play football at recess, but there's only one ball and some other kids always get it first.
12. You're really tall, and other kids make fun of you. You wish you didn't look so different.
13. Your brother seems to be the perfect one in the family. He gets good grades, has a lot of friends, and hardly ever gets in trouble with your parents. You can't help feeling jealous.
14. You studied hard for a test but didn't get a good grade. You think the questions were unfair.
15. You are with a bunch of friends. They all decide to go somewhere your parents don't allow you to go. Your friends say you should go anyway because your parents will never find out.

Problem Situations—Adolescents

These situations are designed for discussion and practice with the seven-step problem-solving model. Most adolescents will have little difficulty with the complexity of the model, but may not have the best judgment in choosing solutions. Provide guidance as necessary, working toward more autonomous functioning. As when working with younger children, introduce obstacles to chosen solutions (for example; if the solution to the first situation is "change to a different class," ask what he would do if the school did not allow him to do that). If the youngster wants to create his own practice situations, he should be encouraged to do so.

1. Your English teacher really seems to have it in for you. You worked all weekend on a paper and got a lower grade than what you think you deserved.
2. You are at a party given by some kids you don't know well, and after you get there you find out that everybody is using drugs. You don't want to participate but they laugh at you for being so "straight."
3. Your body seems to be developing more slowly than for most kids your age, and you feel very embarrassed about it. The worst part is that in the locker room after gym class, the others make fun of you.
4. You usually walk to school and eat lunch with a particular friend. Recently this person has been spending a lot of time with somebody else, and is ignoring you.

5. You are taking a test and the person in front of you turns around while the teacher isn't looking, and looks at your paper. You studied hard for this test and don't feel like sharing your answers. Besides, if the teacher sees this she might think you were helping this person voluntarily.

6. You go to a school dance with some friends. Nobody you'd like to dance with will even look at you.

7. Lately your parents seem to be fighting a lot. It seems like they're taking it out on your younger brother, and you think the punishments they're giving him are unfair.

8. You want to extend your weekend curfew so you can stay out as late as your friends, but your parents are really strict. You feel that they don't give you enough credit for being responsible.

9. Your brothers and sisters are always bothering you when you're at home with some friends. Your parents don't seem to understand how mad this makes you; they say, "It's their house too."

10. Your best friend has started moving in on the person you'd like to go out with. You don't think this is very loyal, and you're upset about it.

11. You would like to be able to go places with your friends, but your allowance won't cover what you want to do. You'd like to get a job, but it would interfere with an important afterschool activity (sports, clubs, etc.) that you don't want to give up.

12. A friend of yours has been acting strange lately. All of a sudden this person doesn't want to do any of the things you used to do together, and basically just wants to sit in his/her room alone all the time. You're upset because you've lost your friend, and you're kind of worried about this person.

13. Your mother never wants you to do anything with your friends, but your father usually lets you. If you just ask your father, your mother gets mad and your parents get in a fight. You want to be able to go out with your friends without causing a family uproar.

14. You're out shopping with a friend, and after you leave the store this person shows you something he/she shoplifted, and suggests you both go back to the store and do it again. You wouldn't mind having a new album for free, but you're afraid of getting caught. You don't want your friend to think you're scared.

15. A friend of yours asks to borrow something of yours. You really don't want to lend this particular item, but this person has loaned you things before and you feel like you should.

HOMEWORK

Ask the child to use the problem-solving steps on a real problem at home or at school at least once before you meet again. Next session, have the child describe the problem she encountered and tell how she used the problem-solving steps. Ask what was easy and hard about the process. Discuss whether the best solution was chosen. If she did not do the homework, work out the steps for a problem she has experienced. It may be necessary to work through more practice situations if the child does not seem fairly comfortable with this process yet. Some children may acquire the cognitive strategies but not yet possess the social skills to implement a solution; in this case, review problem solving again after teaching communication skills (chapter 11).

Chapter 6
Self-Statements

Most of us can think of two very different kinds of conversations we have: the social exchanges we have when we talk to another person and those conversations we have when we talk to ourselves. Private speech, as these conversations with ourselves have been called, can be used for many purposes. In this chapter we focus on how children use self-statements to *describe* themselves, such as when a child says to himself that "nobody likes me," that "I'm stupid," or that "I'm pretty special." We first consider developmental changes in children's private speech and then discuss how the ways in which children talk to themselves may influence their self-esteem. Finally, we present assessment and treatment strategies to help children overcome problems in their use of self-statements. As will become clear in the following chapters, children's use of "self-talk" plays a role in other important domains, including their self-control (chapter 7), attributional styles (chapter 8), and standard setting (chapter 9).

THE DEVELOPMENT OF
PRIVATE SPEECH

Some of our comments in Chapter 3 about developmental changes in children's self-concepts are important in understanding how self-statements may change as children mature. In terms of self-concept, children's thoughts about what they are like begin as *concrete*, absolute, and specific ideas ("I am a boy;" "I have a red bicycle"). The way in which children's concepts mature, however, may make them particularly vulnerable to problems with low self-esteem. As we noted in chapter 3, children's concepts become more *abstract* during the school age years, and in terms of their ideas about what people are like (themselves included) they move from a focus on concrete attributes,

such as physical characteristics or possessions, to interpersonal qualities—friendly, kind, popular (Livesley & Bromley, 1973). These more
abstract qualities, however, have broader-based implications that the
school-aged child begins to recognize. That is, older children are more
likely to *generalize* from one attribute about the self to another ("It's
good to be popular so I must be pretty special"), to include a *temporal*
dimension in their thinking about themselves ("I'm not very popular
now and probably nobody will ever be my friend"), to consider the
consequences of particular attributes ("I'm not very popular so I probably
won't be invited to Joey's birthday party"), and to *compare* themselves
to others ("I'm not as popular as Joey"). These thinking abilities mean
that older children with negative self-concepts may talk to themselves
in a very different way than children with positive self-concepts.

Part of the problem of children during the school-age years is that
they are acquiring certain mental abilities, such as the abilities to think
more abstractly, to generalize, to comprehend time, to understand
cause and consequence, and to engage in social comparisons. Yet other
important capacities, such as the ability to think hypothetically (about
things that may happen in the future or things that do not actually
exist) and to construct more differentiated concepts (ideas that are not
absolute, either/or), are not acquired by some youngsters until late in
adolescence, or perhaps, not at all.

Such *hypothetical thinking abilities*, however, may protect a child's self-
esteem, for instance by allowing him to imagine standards for behavior
that do not presently exist in his peer group. For example, rather than
comparing himself to his classmates and coming up short, a youngster
with more advanced thinking skills might say to himself that he "would
do a lot better in soccer if I didn't have to play against kids who've
been playing since they were five years old." An unpopular child
might try to ignore the contingencies of his daily life at school and tell
herself that "it's more important to be intelligent than to be popular."

Similarly, the ability to construct *differentiated concepts*, as opposed to
the absolutist notions of childhood, may serve to promote more positive
self-concepts. Whereas a younger child may equate one indication of
a characteristic with his overall personality or self-concept ("I got
straight A's so I must be smart"), a youngster with more advanced
thinking abilities may realize that characteristics may be specific to
particular settings or times ("I'm really good at math, but terrible at
spelling;" "I lost my temper this afternoon, but I usually get along
pretty well with my friends;" "At school nobody really notices me, but
at camp the other kids really seemed to like me"). Because a child's
self-concept is determined to a large degree by how others treat him,
it is also important for a child to think in a differentiated way about

other people ("My teacher yelled at me this morning, but usually she seems like she likes me;" "My math teacher doesn't seem to like me at all, but my history teacher does"). In short, part of helping a youngster develop a more positive self-image may involve getting him to talk to himself about what he is like and about how others see him: (a) in a more differentiated way; and (b) with a different set of standards in mind. We discuss standard setting in more detail in chapter 8; in this chapter we focus on helping children see the consequences of how they talk to themselves.

The consequences of children's self-statements for their self-concepts and self-esteem are fairly obvious: a child may generalize from a specific incident or set of circumstances to develop a global and permanent idea (either positive or negative) about what she is like—and her ideas about herself may override any contradictory feedback from other people or from future experiences. As such, a negative self-image may become "set in stone."

Children may use private speech to describe themselves in negative ways because they model or imitate self-descriptions of the important adults in their lives (such as those of a parent who calls himself "a failure"). They also may be used to hearing themselves described in a particular way by adults or other children (for instance, when a parent tells a child he is a "lazy bum" or a "slob" because he hasn't cleaned his room, or when other youngsters tell a child she is "stupid" or "a dumbbell" because she is in the slow learner track in her grade). As we noted earlier, once children develop an idea about what they are like on the basis of how others treat them, they may elaborate on that basic idea and attribute other related characteristics to themselves. Thus, a "lazy bum" may also come to describe himself as "stupid," "no good" and "a failure." In helping children who have low self-esteem, it is important to determine just how children describe themselves. These descriptions often may have no basis in fact, and so an important treatment goal is to teach children to describe themselves in new ways. In the remainder of this chapter, we discuss means of assessing and modifying children's self-descriptions. We also present more general techniques with which to teach children how to use private speech to control their feelings and their behavior.

ASSESSMENT

In this section we describe strategies for determining children's use of self-statements. In each of these areas it is necessary to consider both the child's developmental level—whether she is delayed, on time, or advanced relative to her age-mates, as well as the appropriateness of her private speech (whether her self-directed speech is positive or negative, productive or nonproductive).

Self-Descriptions I

Construct a set of cards on which are printed adjectives that can be used to describe people (see Table 6.1 for a sample list). In addition, you should make four "key cards" on which are printed: (a) exactly like me; (b) a lot like me; (c) sort of like me; (d) not very much like me; (e) not at all like me. Tell the child that you would like to know how he describes himself, and have him sort the adjective cards into piles (represented by the key cards). If the child is older (10 or 11 years or more), have him resort the cards to show (a) how a parent would describe him; (b) how a teacher would describe him; (c) how a friend would describe him. Some children will not make distinctions between their own and others' views of themselves (see chapter 10); only older, more cognitively and socially sophisticated children should be asked to make multiple sorts.

Look for themes in the child's self-evaluations. The adjectives come from six areas that correspond to dimensions of school aged children's self-concepts (self-esteem in academics, peer acceptance, appearance, athletic abilities, conduct and general self-worth). Your goal is to determine whether the child is evaluated negatively in any given area(s) by himself or others. An additional goal is to see whether the child expresses a different perception of himself than he believes others would. As we note in chapter 10, children who believe that everyone sees them in the same way as they see themselves may be functioning at a less mature level of social understanding. Look for large discrepancies in self versus other descriptions, such as when the child evaluates himself positively (sort of like me, like me) and indicates, for example, that a teacher would evaluate him negatively (not very much like me, not at all like me). You can use these areas of negative evaluations by self and other as a basis for reflecting your view of the child's self-image ("It looks like you think you're not real good at sports;" "So you'd say your teacher thinks you don't get along well with the other kids") to gain more information from the child, who may be trying to appear modest or who may want to look good in your eyes. Finally, look for a tendency for a child to evaluate himself in extremes (a lot like me, not at all like me). This may signal a child who has difficulty thinking of himself in non-absolutist (more differentiated) terms—a characteristic of children who may be less mature intellectually.

Self-Descriptions II

Ask the child to describe what he is like, in an open ended way. Note the kinds of descriptors he uses: concrete characteristics or possessions; interpersonal traits (friendly, nice), values, attitudes. Then ask the child to describe himself in the following domains:

1. Academics ("What are you usually like at school?");
2. Sports ("What are you usually like at sports?");
3. Friendships ("What are you usually like with other kids?");
4. Appearance ("What do you usually look like?");
5. Conduct ("How do you usually behave?").

For younger or shy children, such open-ended questions may be difficult to answer; if so, go on to the next activity.

Sentence Completions

The preceding exercises will help you determine whether the child's self-image is positive or negative, as well as whether it is cognitively sophisticated (more abstract and differentiated). The sentence completion strategy is designed to help you determine the extent to which the child actually uses self-descriptors. Say to the child:

> A lot of times when things happen to us or when we do something real good or bad we talk to ourselves. For example, when she gets a good grade on a test, one girl might say to herself, "I'm really good in math;" but another girl might think, "Boy, I was really lucky on that test." Other kids might not think anything special at all. What I'd like to do is to find out what *you* think at certain times or when certain things happen to *you*. I want you to answer these questions as quickly as you can and tell me the first thing that comes to mind. You may not usually say anything to yourself sometimes and you should tell me that too."

Read the following phrases to the child and note her responses.

> When my parents yell at me I say to myself. . . .
> When I make a mistake I think. . . .
> I can't. . . .
> When I get a bad grade I think. . . .
> I'm no good at. . . .
> When my friends get mad at me I say to myself. . . .

When I try but can't do something that other kids can I think. . . .
I worry about. . . .
When I look in the mirror I think. . . .
It would be better if I. . . .
Everybody should. . . .

You should note how spontaneous a child's answers are, or whether it takes the child some time to come up with a response (more spontaneous answers may indicate that the child has had more practice with a particular thought—that is, that she has used it more often).

INTERVENTIONS

In assessment, you will have determined the extent to which a child uses private speech in constructing a negative self-image. Teaching children to use private speech in adaptive ways involves a three step process: (a) helping children *monitor* themselves—either their mental or "covert" activities (such as a tendency to think of themselves in self-deprecating ways); (b) teaching them to *evaluate* their overt or covert behavior (that is, to determine whether their thoughts or behaviors conform to certain standards); and (c) instructing children to *reinforce* themselves for their behavior. We deal with each of these areas, in the following pages.

Identifying Self-Statements I

Explain this aspect of "self-talk" to the child as follows:

We all talk to ourselves inside our heads every day. Lots of times nobody else knows what kinds of things we say to ourselves. In fact, sometimes we don't even notice these little messages that we send to ourselves because they happen so quickly, or because we say the same things so often that it gets to be like a habit. But these little messages are very important, because they can affect the way we feel about ourselves.

Give some examples of self-statements; for example, criticism after making a mistake ("Boy, am I stupid"), or reaction to a slight from a peer ("Everybody hates me"). Focus particularly on areas of negative self-statements which were uncovered during assessment.

As an exercise, use the sentence completions listed in Assessment Exercise 1. Print these on individual index cards and give them to the child. Explain that these are some common things people say to themselves, and that they may be helpful in finding out about some of the child's own self-statements. Again, encourage the child to react quickly rather than think carefully about his response.

Examples:
I'm no good at. . . .
Everybody should. . . .
When somebody gets mad at me I say to myself. . . .
I worry about. . . .
It would be better if I. . . .
When I get a bad grade I think. . . .
I can't. . . .

Record the child's answers as she responds. Going back over the sentence completions from the assessment session will help to give you an idea about the significance of a child's negative self-statements. That is, you will be able to get a sense of which statements may be genuine and stable and which simply may be responses to the exercise. When all sentences are completed, review her answers and ask her when she finds herself sending these messages to herself. Ask about the feelings associated with each of these messages. Try to determine which of these represent actual self-statements (automatic, habitual responses to certain situations) and which were just a response to the exercise.

Explain that many self-statements are accompanied by bad feelings, and that they often make a situation seem much worse than it really is.

For example, if somebody in your class is teasing you, it's only natural to feel bad. But if this situation causes you to send a message to yourself saying "everybody hates me," you're going to feel really terrible. That's why it's important to learn how to "argue away" self-statements that make you feel bad. What you can do is try to talk yourself out of believing the self-statement. So if you're saying "everybody hates me," one way to argue it away is to think that only one person was teasing you, and you do have friends who are usually nice to you. In other words, maybe one person doesn't like you, but that doesn't mean EVERYBODY hates you. Or maybe this person was just in a mean mood today, and doesn't hate you at all. The important thing to remember is that you don't have to believe the message in your head, especially if it's one that makes you feel a lot worse than you should in a situation. Arguing away self-statements takes practice. It seems very unnatural at first, and it might not even work at all the first few times you try it. But if you keep doing it, eventually you'll find that it gets easier and easier to argue away the message and the bad feelings that go along with it, and the message itself might stop coming up so often.

When the child understands the concept of arguing away self-statements, go back to the sentence completions that appeared to be genuine self-statements, and work on arguments for them. Stress that each person has to create her own arguments, because something that works for one person might not work for another. If she has trouble with this, suggest some possible arguments, but be sure that she has an opportunity to think about whether they are likely to work for her. *It is especially important for the child to be involved in changing her self-statements*; in fact, if the youngster can discover alternative statements herself, permanent changes are more likely to be obtained. Talk about situations that are likely to elicit these self-statements, and have the child imagine being in the situations, experiencing the self-statements and the related feelings, and then arguing them away.

For *homework*, in preparation for the next session, ask the child to monitor her self-statements and notice the situations when they arise. Remind her that self-statements are often hard to find at first, and that bad feelings are a clue that a message has just gone through your head. Ask her to notice if she finds any new self-statements that were not discussed in this session. Suggest that she might want to try arguing away any self-statements that she finds.

In the following session, review the homework. What self-statements did she find? Were they ones you discussed in the last session, or new ones? What was happening when she discovered the self-statements? How did she know that's what they were? What feelings did she have at the time? Did she try to argue them away? Did it work? What might be some effective arguments?

Identifying Self-Statements II

Again, you will be using one of the procedures described in Assessment, this time the cards with self descriptive adjectives. First, give the child the index cards on which are printed the negative self-descriptors. Ask him to choose labels he has used on himself at any time, even if it doesn't happen very often. Ask about situations where this happens, feelings associated with it, and more elaborate self-statements that might be related to the label. Notice if there seem to be any themes to the child's collection of self-statements by seeing if the negative self-descriptors fall in a particular category and/or if the child chooses the same negative descriptors as in the assessment exercise. If so, talk about these with the child to see if these are difficult areas for him. If a cluster of self-statements compose a *theme* (for instance, problems in domains such as academics, athletics, peer relations or appearance), explain that it is even more important to argue them away because of the potential for a lot of bad feelings to arise around this area. Work carefully on constructing arguments for each self-statement found, being sure that the child feels that each argument could be effective. Remember that children with different levels of cognitive sophistication will be persuaded by different kinds of reasons. For instance, younger children will tend to respond to arguments about concrete consequences or statements about accuracy and inaccuracy, whereas older youngsters will respond to more abstract or hypothetical rationales.

Self Reinforcement for Positive Self-Statements

After the child has learned to monitor his self-statements and to evaluate his behavior, he needs to learn to reinforce himself when he uses positive self-statements or when he "argues away" negative ones. Model strategies to the child by presenting him with vignettes about potentially distressing circumstances:

EXAMPLES:

A. The teacher yells at you in class and you respond by thinking, "She doesn't like me," and feeling hurt.

Show how the child can argue away these ideas and feelings by, for instance, thinking of times the teacher has shown she likes him, or thinking of other examples of the teacher's yelling which might prove that the teacher was in a bad mood that day. Then model *self-reinforcement* by saying: "I did a good job thinking about why Mr. B. really yelled at me—I feel much better now."

B. You don't get invited to a party even though most of the other kids in the class are going, and you respond by thinking, "Nobody likes me," and feeling bad.

Show how you can argue away these ideas and feelings by thinking about the other people who are really important to you (your family, a best friend) or about how you may be different from the other kids in positive ways (e.g., "those kids seem to get into trouble a lot—they don't seem to be really interested in reading and learning like I am"). Then model self-reinforcement by saying "I remembered to think about how I talk to myself and I thought of some good ways to make myself feel better. I'm pretty good at this."

For homework have the child practice self-reinforcement and, in the following session, discuss his strategies with him. You may want to encourage him to reward himself tangibly at times for a day's or week's worth of self-monitoring and evaluation. Seeing a movie, buying a candy bar, staying up later one night to watch a TV show, or playing a game or going for a soda during one treatment session with the child may be means of rewarding long-term use of appropriate self-talk. Remember, it is also important for you to provide positive feedback to the child for her attempts and successes at changing her self-statements; your praise is a significant part of the change program.

TABLE 6.1. Personal Attributes

honest (P) _____	neat & clean (C) _____
sloppy (C) _____	helpful (I) _____
friendly (I) _____	boring (I) _____
polite (I) _____	selfish (I) _____
lazy (C) _____	good-looking (C) _____
bossy (I) _____	mean (I) _____
smart (C) _____	clumsy (C) _____
rich (C) _____	happy _____
nice (I) _____	religious (P) _____
curious (C) _____	good at sports _____
fat (C) _____	conservative (P) _____

Attributes may be categorized as indicators of concrete characteristics of a person's physical appearance or behavior (C), interpersonal characteristics (I), or principles and values (P).

Chapter 7
Attributional Style

An attribution explains an event by relating it to a cause. We employ them to explain the causes for the things that happen to us. Attributions generally take the form of self-statements; they function as a type of self-speech, as discussed in chapter 6. That is, "in our heads," on a repeated basis in our lives, we ascribe or attribute causes to specific events.

As with self-speech, we may not always be aware of this attribution process; however, attributions are not unconscious. If we focus our attention on them we can know what our attributions are. Also like private speech, attributions, do, in general, affect how we feel. They can make us feel bad in a situation in which we deserve to feel good, or they can make us feel worse than we need to in a bad situation. Finally, like self-statements, we have a choice about the types of attributions we make. An individual can, therefore, change his attributions as a type of cognitive modification. Many times this will also result in behavioral and emotional change. For every event we have a choice of several different explanations. Sometimes the explanations or attributions we choose are good for us, but at other times they unnecessarily make us feel bad.

There are several dimensions of attributions; these include *situation*, *time*, and *locus of control* (see Abramson, Seligman, & Teasdale, 1978). They suggested that there are different types of attributions for each dimension. Situational attributions may be global or specific. *Global* attributions generalize beyond a specific situation, and attribute the cause of the event to many other events in one's life. A *specific* attribution limits the conclusion about causality to the specific, current situation. Temporal attributions may be stable or unstable. *Stable* attributions perceive the cause of the situation or event as representative of many that have occurred in the past and will occur again in the future. *Unstable* attributions perceive the cause of this event as an isolated one that has not happened previously and is unlikely to happen again. Locus of control

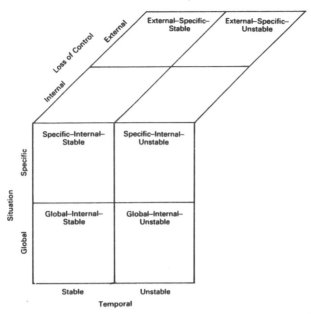

FIGURE 7.1. Dimensions and types of attributions. Based on "Learned Helplessness in Humans: Critique and Reformulation," by L. Y. Abramson, M. E. Seligman, and J. Teasdale, 1978, *Journal of Abnormal Psychology, 87,* 49–74.

can be either internal or external. *Internal* attributions ascribe the cause of an event to yourself. *External* attributions are made when the individual ascribes the cause for the event as being beyond that person's control; the control is external to the individual to whom the event is happening. These types of attributions are presented in Figure 7.1.

An attribution may represent all of these dimensions; thus, we speak of an attibution as being global-stable-internal, specific-stable-internal, and so on. If a person regularly uses a pattern of dimensions for her attributions, that is called an *attributional style.* For example, Abramson, Seligman, and Teasdale (1978) suggested an attributional style characteristic of depressed individuals. They posited that a depressed person makes internal–stable–global attributions for negative events and external–unstable–specific attributions for positive events. Numerous research studies have shown that depressed adults and children exhibit this specific attributional style (Peterson & Seligman, 1984; Seligman & Peterson, 1986). Since low self-esteem and depression are highly correlated in children and adolescents (Craighead & Green, 1987), low self-esteem youngsters appear to use this "depressive attributional style." It remains to be demonstrated how various other types of attributional styles may be related to specific psychological disorders.

Since we make attributions about all kinds of negative and positive events, there are many possible examples of attributions and attributional style. One of the most frequently used examples is failing a math test. Possible types of attributions for failing the math test would be:

Situation
> Global   "I fail the tests because I do not do well on any exams."
> Specific   "I did poorly on this test because I'm not good on math tests."

Time
> Stable   "I did poorly on this test because I always do poorly on math tests."
> Unstable "I did poorly on this test because I did not feel well today."

Locus of Control
> Internal   "I did poorly on the math test because I'm no good at math."
> External   "I did poorly on the math test because there was so much noise in the room I could not concentrate."

Most attributions involve more than one dimension at a time, an attributional style. The following is an example of attributions in all possible combinations from the various dimensions for a child who has been rejected by a classmate. This example may be applied to a number of social situations involving children and adolescents.

	Internal	
	Stable	*Unstable*
Global	Nobody likes me.	Sometimes others don't think I'm fun to be with.
Specific	This person doesn't like me.	This person doesn't think I'm fun to be with.

	External	
	Stable	*Unstable*
Global	Some kids just like to be mean and pick on others.	Sometimes kids get into a mean mood.
Specific	This person likes to pick on others.	This person was in a mean mood today.

Attributions are important because they are a type of self-statement cognition that fits in the social learning model. The way we attribute the causes of events has an affect on how we feel, behave, and think. Attributions, therefore, play a major role in how a child evaluates his or her self concept.

ASSESSMENT OF ATTRIBUTIONS

In order to assess the child's attributional pattern, you can use the sentence completion items noted in Chapter 6.[1] Pay careful attention to the types of attributions the child makes in completing the following sentences. Read the following phrases to the child and note her response.

When my parents yell at me I say to myself . . .
When I make a mistake I think . . .
I can't . . .
When I get a bad grade I think . . .
I'm no good at . . .
When my friends get mad at me I say to myself . . .
When I try but can't do something that other kids can, I think . . .
I worry about . . .
When I look in the mirror I think . . .
It would be better if I . . .
Everybody should . . .

Note how general, permanent, and internal a child's attributions are; for instance, "when I get a bad grade I think: 'I'm stupid,' " rather than " 'I should have studied more.' " Finally, determine how much self-blame is evident ("I should have studied more" versus "That teacher makes up stupid tests"). It is important to find out whether the child spontaneously uses such self-statements as these in his day-to-day activities, and you should question him about this by asking: "Do you usually say _____ to yourself when you get a bad grade on a test, or do you usually just go on to something else?", and "How do you feel when you

---

[1] The most widely used standardized, assessment instrument to evaluate children's attributions is the Children's Attributional Style Questionnaire (CASQ). It has also been called the KASTAN. It is composed of 48 items which are pairs of statements reflecting dimensions of attributions. A positive or negative event is listed, and the child is offered two alternatives (e.g. global or specific, stable or unstable, internal or external) for attributing a cause to the event. The scale has been standardized, so you can determine an attributional style from the score. A child can score high on any combination of dimensions of attributions. The test provides a score for both positive and negative events. You can use the CASQ to get a total attributional style score. You also can use it as an example of attributions. For example, the individual items may be viewed as samples of the types of attributions, so you may have many first-hand samples of the child's way of thinking about causes for events. The CASQ is available for professional use from Dr. Martin E. P. Seligman, Department of Psychology, University of Pennsylvania, 3815 Walnut Street, Philadelphia, PA, 19104.

say _____ to yourself when you get a bad grade?" Children who use very *general* or *global* negative self-statements, who attribute *blame* to themselves, who do so on a regular basis, and who give rise to negative emotion when they do so, clearly are in greater need of intervention in this area.

MODIFICATION OF ATTRIBUTIONS

In order for a youngster to change his attributions, it is important that he understands what attributions are, and how they function as self-statements to influence other private speech and all other domains of human functioning. Furthermore, it is important for the child to understand the dimensions of attributions, what they are, and how they are organized.

Children of the developmental level we are talking about best understand attributions when they are given a few concrete examples which are relevant to them. Following the examples in the first section of this chapter, you should help the child generate attributions for relevant events in her life.

Once the child has a good feel for the dimensions of attributions and how they interact (see Figure 7.1), then you can begin to change the attributional style. Ask the child for one good event and one bad event that has recently happened to her. For each event, think of a reasonable example of each type of attribution. Sometimes the same explanation will be applicable to more than one type of attribution. You may have to do one example entirely by yourself until the child begins to understand the meaning of the different types of attributions.

Here are some examples of attributions for a good and bad event.

Event: I won a drawing contest.
Global:	I'm good at drawing.
Specific:	I drew one good picture.
Stable:	I always draw good pictures.
Unstable:	I drew a good picture that time.
Internal:	I'm good at drawing.
External:	I got lucky.

Event: Kids tease me.
Global:	Nobody likes me.
Specific:	The kids who tease me don't like me.
Stable:	These kids don't like me.
Unstable:	These kids were being mean today.

Internal: I must be weird since they tease me.
External: They were mad about something else and took it out on me.

When doing these examples, make sure that the attributions given are either accurate or plausible for the child's experience of the events. Write down the attributions for each event. When both are completed, ask the child which attributions she made at the time. Did they make her feel good or bad? Which of the attributions listed would result in good feelings? Which would result in bad feelings?

Explain that attributions are a type of self-statement. They can make you feel bad in a situation where you deserve to feel good, or they can make you feel worse in a bad situation. Like self-statements, you have a choice about what you believe. After doing several more examples, lead the child to the conclusion that global, internal, and stable attributions result in good feelings in positive situations, and specific, external, and unstable attributions result in good (better) feelings in negative situations. The general rule for positive situations is to take credit for your successes, not to explain them away. The general rule for negative situations is to decide realistically if you can correct the situation or prevent it from happening again; if not, explain away the bad feelings. You may have to help an extremely self-critical child with that for which she can realistically take responsibility.

Homework for the next session is to think about one good event and one bad event that happened recently (preferably during the time between sessions) and think about all six types of attributions for each one. Discuss this in the next session. If the child is having trouble convincing herself to believe the most constructive attributions, help her to develop better (more believable) attributions. If she seems to be using reasonable attributions but still has trouble believing the ones she should, reassure her that she should still try to convince herself of the constructive ones and that it will become easier with time.

As with any type of self-statements or thoughts, the objective is for the youngster to substitute adaptive ones for maladaptives ones. As the individual repeats and comes to *believe* the more adaptive attributional style, her self-esteem will rise because over time and situations she comes to accept responsibility for positive events and stops blaming herself for negative events.

Chapter 8
Self-Control

In chapter 3, we noted that children's self-control abilities represent one of the three components of the self-system. Self-control appears to be a factor in children's positive self-esteem because children who can control their own emotions and behavior feel more competent. In addition, children who exhibit self-control may be evaluated positively by others, including their teachers, parents, and even peers, whereas those who behave impulsively or lose their tempers frequently may be seen in a more negative light.

In our discussions of self-statements (chapter 6) and attributional style (chapter 7) we found that the ways in which children talk to themselves can influence their self-esteem. Similarly, children's self-control abilities appear to rest, at least in part, on whether and how they talk to themselves. Whereas poor self-esteem seems to be caused by children's *inappropriate use* of self-statements and attributions, deficiencies in self-control often appear to arise from children's *failure* to use private speech.

THE DEVELOPMENT OF SELF-TALK
FOR SELF-CONTROL

The way children's private speech guides their behavior changes as children develop. As we noted in chapter 3, children initially talk to themselves out loud, and only after they reach about six or seven years of age is private speech really private—that is, "internalized" as thought (Meacham, 1979). And, it takes even longer for children to realize the effectiveness of private speech and to deliberately use cognitive control—or "thought control"—over their behavior. Such cognitive control includes such mental activities as *rationalizing* a mistake to avoid self-blame and maintain one's self-esteem as when children make attributions about the causes of events (e.g., "That test had a lot of stupid questions and that's why I flunked it."), or, alternatively, when they develop negative *self-fulfilling prophecies* which can lead to increased failure ("I'm so slow I'll *never* be able to finish this test on time"). Children also use private speech to *plan* (for instance, how they will handle a social situation) or to *control impulsive reactions* (for instance, a quick temper that alienates other children and adult from the child and may lead to social rejection).

The Developmental Significance of Self-Control

As we have suggested, an important consequence of children's acquisition of self-guiding speech is the potential this activity provides for children to control their own experiences. When children become able to develop plans for their activities and strategies for achieving their goals, they become capable—as some researchers have put it—of "producing their own development" (Lerner & Busch-Rossnagel, 1981). That is, they acquire more "say" in what activities and experiences they will be exposed to, and in how those activities turn out. Children with strong impulse control may be seen by themselves and others as more mature and responsible, and thus acquire more positive self-images. In addition, these children may be given more leeway about choosing and participating in activities that will maximize their chances of receiving positive feedback from their environment, experiences which in turn will support their positive self-concepts. Private speech is certainly not enough to ensure that a child will take control of her activities and experiences to maximize the positive feedback she receives, but this ability does seem to be one important factor.

Individual Differences in the Development of Self-Control

Some studies have shown that children of the same chronological age may be very different in their use of private speech. For instance, two separate lines of research have shown that children's performance and the feedback they receive, both in the classroom and in social interactions with other children, may vary, at least in part, because children differ in how they talk to themselves.

Why do children with the same IQ's show such different levels of academic achievement? This question was at the root of a set of studies which investigated children's "cognitive styles" (Kagan, Rosman, Day, Albert, & Phillips, 1964). This research showed that two groups of children could be identified: (a) *reflective* youngsters, who tend to work slowly and carefully on analytic tasks in school, and who make fewer mistakes in their work; and (b) *impulsive* youngsters, who, as this label suggests, go quickly through the tasks they are assigned at school—and make more mistakes.

Clearly, a child with an impulsive style may show lower levels of learning at school—and will receive more negative feedback about her abilities, even though she may be as capable as other children. Not only will such experiences limit her intellectual growth, but to the extent to which doing well in school is important to the child, her parents, or the peer group, the child's self-esteem may suffer.

To help children overcome problems with impulsivity on academic tasks, researchers have tested the effectiveness of procedures designed to teach children to talk to themselves in different ways as they are working on their school work. As with the social problem solving strategies discussed in chapter 5, children are taught to stop and think about the problem (or task). Specifically, children may be taught to explore the features of the problem—that is, to analyze it in a careful and systematic way, to plan the problem solution, to carry out that plan, and to reinforce themselves for going through this process. *Self-instructions* ("Remember to read through the whole question"; "Go back to check your work"), modeled by adults and then role-played by the child (first out loud, then covertly), guide the child's behavior in this process.

Another group of children whose private speech seems to be different from that of their age-mates is impulsive-aggressive children. We described how these children can be taught to talk to themselves in social problem solving in chapter 5. One important discovery by researchers about these children's self-statements, however, has to do with how they interpret others' behavior. Specifically, impulsive-aggressive boys are more likely to think that accidental injuries caused by other children actually are done on purpose (Dodge & Frame, 1982). Consequently, they are more likely to retaliate in an aggressive way than are other youngsters their age. This can make them less popular with their peers and also can cause them to be disliked by teachers or other adults. We discussed children's attributions—their ideas about the causes of their own and others' behavior—in greater detail in chapter 7. The important point, however, is that the way children talk to themselves can have a profound effect on their behavior, and in turn, because of the social feedback they receive, on their self-esteem. Teaching children to talk to themselves in new ways is often an effective means of dealing with these problems. In the remainder of the chapter, we consider means of assessing and modifying children's use of self-talk in controlling their feelings and behaviors.

Assessment

Children may use private speech for self-control without really being aware of it. Developing an awareness of different kinds of strategies, however, may enable children deliberately to choose an effective strategy in situations where they need to control their behavior. Present the following situations to the child and ask for her ideas about how she would try to control her behavior. For younger children, open-ended questions may be too difficult and you may need to provide choices of more and less sophisticated self-control strategies for the child to select.

1. Suppose your mother had told you that you were not allowed to have any cookies before dinner. If you were really hungry and really liked the cookies what would you do? Is there anything you could do to keep from eating some of the cookies? (Possible responses: Put them away in a cabinet so I couldn't see them; tell myself I could eat them after dinner.)
2. Suppose your father told you that your friend couldn't sleep over at your house that night. What would you do? Is there anything you could do to keep from feeling angry or unhappy? (Possible responses: Go out and play or go read a book so I could forget about it; Make a plan for a sleep-over on some other night.)
3. Suppose you had a lot of homework to do and your brother or sister was watching your favorite show on television. What would you do? Is there anything you could do to keep yourself from watching the show? (Possible responses: Think that I'd be able to watch the show next week; Work up in my room where I couldn't hear the program.)
4. Suppose some kids in your class were goofing around and one kid whom you don't really like got pushed and banged his elbow into your head. If you got hurt badly you might feel like hurting him/her right back. What would you do? Is there anything you could do to keep from hitting him/her right back? (Possible answers: Tell myself it was an accident and hurting the other kid wouldn't be nice; Close my eyes and count to 10 so I would stop feeling angry.)

When evaluating children's spontaneous self-control strategies, note the extent to which the child knows to distract herself and the extent to which she uses mental means (for instance, transforming an event in her mind) to control her behavior. Of course, you also will need to know just how a child behaves in these potentially challenging situations. You can talk to children about their actual behavior in situations such as these, as well as getting input from teachers or parents about the extent to which self-control is a significant problem for a child.

Intervention

Children may display very different kinds of self-control problems. Some may have difficulty inhibiting their impulses or emotions in social situations, some may complete academic tasks in a manner that makes them appear careless, still other children may believe they have very little control over themselves and their behavior (that is, they have an *external locus of control*). Children may have problems in one or more of these areas. As such, the results of assessments should be considered carefully in choosing among the activities described in the following pages.

Explaining self-control. Say to the child: "Most of the time parents or teachers or even older kids tell little children what to do and make sure they don't get into trouble. The older you get, though, the more you have to tell youself what to do and how to behave. One way that older people get themselves to do what they know they should is to talk to themselves. Today we're going to learn how people can talk to themselves in different ways so that they will behave the way that you want.'

Explain that you will be talking about three situations in which people talk to themselves to control their behavior:

1. To keep themselves from doing things they shouldn't (*inhibition*), such as when one resists temptation or delays gratification of a desire (for instance, not eating forbidden candy or waiting till after supper to eat the candy), or controls the expression of their emotions;
2. To decide what they should do in certain situations (*planning*) such as when they need to carry out a task involving several steps;
3. To *maintain* their involvement in a task over a period of time without being distracted or reducing the quality of their performance.

Give examples to the child of situations requiring self-control and ask the child to describe what some of the consequences may be for failure to exhibit self-control. Then ask the child to come up with her own examples of situations that require self-control.

Examples:
Inhibition: When another child makes you angry such as by hitting or teasing you or taking something that belongs to you.
When you want to ask the teacher a question during class.
When your parents have told you that you aren't allowed to watch a TV program you like.
When you know you're not supposed to eat sweets before dinner.

Planning: Doing chores at home.

Doing a homework assignment or project.

Buying presents for family members (such as at Christmas or Hanukkah).

Planning a birthday party or class party.

Planning a trip or outing.

Maintenance: Completing a homework or class assignment.

Engaging in athletic activity (running, bike riding, or other activity requiring endurance).

Doing chores.

Understanding rules. Part of self-control involves knowing the rules to which one's behavior should conform. Begin by talking to the child about rules—why we have them and what would happen if we did not. Have the child tell you one or two rules from home or school that she knows and talk about what would happen if people did not follow those rules. When relevant, talk about the different ways a person could conform to a rule and about what sometimes makes it hard to obey that rule.

Examples:
1. Going to bed at a certain time;
2. Getting parents' permission before going to visit friends;
3. Taking turns with materials at school:
4. Returning library books when they're done.

When interviewing parents and teachers during assessment, you should find out what some of the significant rules are for home and for the classroom. Review these with the child. Ask her first to describe the rule(s) for a certain area of activity. (For instance, "Can you tell me what the rule is for talking out loud during class?"). If the child cannot answer, give her a choice of two possible rules ("Is the rule that you can talk whenever the teacher is not talking, or that you can talk when you raise your hand and the teacher calls on you?"). With these rules as well, discuss the consequences of rule disobedience, the possible ways of conforming to a given rule, and the difficulty of following certain rules.

Understanding social scripts. "Script" is a term given to a conventional pattern of social interaction, such as making introductions or taking a telephone message. In a sense, scripts are rules for social interaction. Part of self-control involves a child's awareness of these social conventions: In order to regulate his behavior in accordance with social conventions, a child first must be aware of what those conventions are.

Explain to the child that in certain situations, most people usually behave in certain ways, and that you are going to practice some of these ways of doing things by playing the parts of people in different situations.

Take turns planning each role so that you can model appropriate behavior to the child and give the child feedback on his behavior.

Examples:
1. Someone calls on the phone and gets the wrong number;
2. Someone calls on the phone for a family member and you have to take a message;
3. Someone accidentally bumps you or runs into you;
4. You approach a group of children playing and want to be included in their game;
5. You buy some candy at the store;
6. You interrupt two adults talking to ask one of them a question;
7. You ask a stranger for directions;
8. You greet a friend you have not seen for some time.

Making and following plans. Talk to the child about the value of making and following plans. Explain how when someone has a number of things she has to do, she can think about these things ahead of time and decide: what needs to be done to accomplish a goal; how she will carry out each task; and in what order she will do them. Making plans can help get everything done correctly and more quickly. Go through some examples of planned versus unplanned situations or experiences.

Examples:
1. You are buying presents for your family (for Christmas, Hanukkah). Because you haven't planned what to get each person, you run out of money before you get a present for everybody.
2. You are going shopping for your birthday party. Because you haven't made a plan, you forget to buy candles for the birthday cake.
3. Your father says you have to finish your homework before you watch your favorite TV show. Because you haven't made a plan, you forget till the last minute about the math problems that have to be handed in tomorrow.

Ask the child to give examples of times that she should have made a plan but did not, and what the consequences were. Ask her to describe what plan she would have made, focusing (when relevant to the situation) on *what* needed to be done, *how* each part should be done, and the *order* in which each part should be accomplished. Give the child feedback on her plan by asking her what would have happened if certain parts of the plan had not been done or if additional parts had been added; what would have happened if any part had been done differently; and what would have happened if she had done things in a different order.

As an example you can talk about planning a slumber party. This might involve (a) inviting friends to the party; (b) shopping for food; and (c) cleaning the child's bedroom in preparation for her guests. A discussion of how each part of the plan is carried out would involve making decisions about whether the child should telephone her friends, talk to them at school, or send them invitations (and the advantages and disadvantages of each strategy). When you talk about the order in which she should carry out her plan, you can point out, for example, that the child would not know for sure what food to buy if she did not know how many friends were coming to her party.

Devise a plan that the child can carry out during the next few days (for instance, planning the most efficient routine for getting ready for school in the morning or planning a special weekend breakfast in bed for mom or dad). For *homework*, have the child carry out the plan and report in the next session on its effectiveness. At that time, you can discuss the importance of making sure your plans meet with the needs and expectations of others around you. Also important to talk about is the way effective plans may bring the child some autonomy and independence— when parents or teachers see that the child is capable of being in charge of her own activities.

Emotion management. Another aspect of self-control involves regulating the intensity and expression of emotion. Inappropriate forms of emotional expression, such as displays of extreme anger or frustration, may result in problems in children's interpersonal relationships or social ostracism; high levels of anxiety or tension can interfere with children's ability to perform in school or sports activities, for example. Thus, children with problems in emotional control may require special intervention efforts.

For children who manifest high levels of anxiety, relaxation training procedures have been developed to teach individuals how to relax their bodies thoroughly while remaining mentally alert (see Bernstein & Borkovec, 1973). This usually is done by alternately tensing and relaxing each of the major muscle groups in the body. A thorough description of the procedures used in progressive muscle relaxation is beyond the scope of this book. Moreover, when children are experiencing extremely high levels of anxiety, a more comprehensive treatment program by an anxiety management expert may be in order. Although those children suffering from clinical anxiety may be experiencing self-control problems, the treatment strategies outlined in this volume are likely to be insufficient to address such problems, and ineffective when applied in the absence of individual professional help.

For children who occasionally have minor difficulties in controlling their emotions or who express their emotions in socially inappropriate ways, one set of procedures that may be used to help children regulate their emotions is based on Novaco's (1978) work on "anger manage-ment." Although the procedures described by Novaco are frequently used to help individuals who experience anger responses, they may be effectively employed with individuals to help them deal with ways of expressing other kinds of emotional responses in socially acceptable ways. In the following examples, we focus on the control of anger; similar procedures may be used to deal with mild levels of frustration or anxiety, as well.

The basic procedure is similar to Differential Affect Training, which we will describe in more detail in chapter 10. Ask the child to identify various gradations of anger which he experiences, beginning with "neutral," at the non-angry end all the way to "rage," or whatever word he uses to describe his highest degree of anger. Make a list of his feeling labels. Next, talk with him about the bodily sensations associated with each label (see Feeling Identification, chapter 5). It is crucial that the child be able to specify three to four progressive stages of anger and to clearly identify the internal feelings that go along with each.

Next ask the child to describe some situations where he might become angry (or past situations which have been problematic for him because of anger). Have him talk about the chronology of the various stages of anger in these situations. When and how does he first notice becoming a little angry? What makes the anger increase? At this point, use the problem-solving steps described in chapter 5, to help the child think of things he could do when he notices the initial stage of anger so that he can avoid getting even more angry. Some alternatives might involve the strategies outlined later in this chapter. It might be enough to discuss new ways of handling these situations, and then direct the child to try them out at home or school. Always encourage children to begin with less difficult situations. The key to managing any mild level of emotion is to help children learn the bodily cues which signal the beginning of their feelings, so that they can take the appropriate steps to avoid losing control of their behavior, as may occur when they are overwhelmed by their feelings. As always, practice outside the session followed by a dis-cussion of how it went is critical for success.

Strategies for self-control. Explain to the child that there are times when most people feel like doing things they should not: yelling at or hitting somebody when you're angry; playing or watching TV when you should be doing your homework or chores; or eating candy when you know it's almost time for dinner. Tell him that in this session you will show him some things he can do to help keep himself from doing things he should not.

Rule verbalization involves repeating to yourself (thinking about) a prohibition or rule for appropriate behavior ("No, I won't yell"; "It's not nice to hit"; "It's time to do homework").

Cognitive restructuring involves mentally altering a situation to make a forbidden behavior or activity less tempting ("That TV show is probably going to be a rerun'; "Those candies really are just buttons—I can imagine mom sewing them on my coat").

Children can also learn to *distract* themselves (such as by going outside to play when they feel like snacking before dinner, or removing the tempting candies from sight).

Another strategy is for children to focus their *attention on the rewards* that will result if they engage in appropriate behavior or the *negative consequences* of behaving inappropriately.

Ask the child to describe some examples of situations in which he is tempted to do things he should not, and model appropriate self-control strategies, using spoken language rather than internalized speech for "thinking strategies" of self-control:

Role-playing. In this session, the child should act out possible self-control strategies in response to different kinds of problematic situations. For thinking strategies (rule verbalization, cognitive restructuring) have the child begin by using spoken language. After he has mastered this step, have him whisper his self-directed communications, and finally have him simply think through those communications in his head. Tell the child to make sure he actually says the whole statement to himself.

For *homework*, have the child keep track of any naturally occurring situations in which he has needed self-control, and what strategies he used to maintain it. He also should be prepared to talk about situations in which he was *unable* to control his bahavior. Review these and help the child come up with ways he might have responded effectively to in these situations.

Self-reinforcement. The final step in helping children use private speech successfully is to teach them how to reinforce themselves when they employ such strategies. Explain to the child that it is important for her to remind herself when she has done a good job in planning, carrying out an activity, or keeping herself from doing things she shouldn't. Model self-reinforcement for these three kinds of situations ("I did a good job coming up with that plan"; "I worked real hard at concentrating while I did my homework;" "I was angry but I reminded myself not to hit—good work!"). Then provide the child with situations and have her role play appropriate self-control strategies and reinforce herself for using effective strategies. Talk about how self-reinforcement makes you feel good because you recognize your accomplishments.

For *homework* ask the child to reinforce herself when she uses private speech strategies and to keep track of these situations. Talk about each situation during the next session, and congratulate her for remembering to reinforce herself.

Chapter 9

Standard Setting

When we experience an event as a "success" or as a "failure," we are measuring our performance against an inner standard. Sometimes standards are very explicit: for example, getting all As or Bs on a report card or making the varsity soccer team. Other standards may be less clear-cut. In fact, we often carry with us internalized expectations for ourselves that may not even enter our awareness. When this happens, there is a potential for us to feel uncomfortable or dissatisfied with ourselves without even knowing why. This may be especially true when our standards are too stringent, resulting in frequently feeling disappointed with ourselves. Clearly, the way we manage our standards for our behavior will have an impact on self-esteem.

In chapter 2, we discussed the four domains of the social learning model (Behavioral, Cognitive, Biological, and Emotional) and their effect on self-esteem. When working with standard setting, the domains of behavior, cognition, and affect (emotions) are involved. Behavior is of concern because it is the behavioral performance which is evaluated. The performance could be in almost any area of life: social relationships, athletic endeavours, academics, hobbies. As we mentioned in chapter 4, it is often helpful to identify the components of self-esteem which are problematic for the child; this information may lead you to areas where his standards are unnecessarily strict. Of course, it is possible that the child's standards are reasonable and a self-esteem problem comes from a lack of appropriate skills. In this situation, the focus must be placed on improving the skill level—for example, through use of chapter 11, Communication Skills, to enhance social relations, or by arranging for tutoring or remedial assistance to improve academic skills.

In addition to the behavioral performance aspect, standard setting involves two kinds of cognitions which may be targets for intervention. First, there is the standard itself, which may be implicit or explicit. That is, the child may find it easy to tell you exactly which levels of performance are acceptable or unacceptable. School grades often fall into this category, because the performance feedback is concrete and clear-cut. Other times, a child may not even realize he used certain standards; these are more difficult to identify and modify. The second type of cognition is the self-evaluation that results from measuring a behavioral performance against a standard. This cognition—which may take the form of a self-statement or an attribution—may be thought of as the conclusion the child draws from the experience of either meeting or missing a standard; as such, it is the mechanism by which performance affects self-esteem. For example, in response to a "success," does the child take credit for doing well ("I did a good job on the math test") or minimize it ("So what if I got a good grade, everybody else did too")? When failing to meet a standard, is the child harsh ("I never win races because I'm just a lousy athlete") or forgiving ("If I keep practicing maybe I'll win next time—at least I tried")? Children can best increase self-esteem by taking credit for successes but minimizing responsibility for failures. In assessing and treating the standards of children with low self-esteem, it is necessary to address both types of cognition: the standard itself, and the reaction to success or failure.

Finally, emotions are involved in standard setting. Following the behavioral performance, the measuring against the standard, and the interpretation of success or failure, there is often an affective response. The child may feel elated or satisfied if he has performed in line with his standards and has given himself credit for doing so. If he has discounted a good performance, such positive feelings will be minimal or absent. In response to a failure experience, the child might have feelings ranging from mild disappointment to shame or self-hatred. These feelings can be diagnostic of the way a child handles performance evaluation, and can be used in an initial assessment—as well as in day-to-day operation—to signal the need for an alternative cognitive strategy. While not a true target of intervention here, emotions are a valuable tool for self-monitoring, and the child should be encouraged to "tune in" to his feelings.

DEVELOPMENTAL CHANGES IN STANDARD SETTING

Initially, standards for our behavior are established by others. Parents of a young child greet certain behaviors with praise, while other efforts fall short of their expectations. Later, teachers make very definite attempts to instill certain standards in their students. When children develop a peer network, their friends influence their ideas about adequate and inadequate performance in various areas. The expanding social environment of the developing child provides for more, and potentially more variable, models and sources of standards and also feedback about how well a child meets those standards. In the midst of these outside influences, children eventually internalize a set of standards for their own performance.

While the expanding social environment provides more models and sources of feedback for children's standards, developmental changes in the child also mean that she will interpret her experiences (for instance, at success and failure) in different ways. For the young (preschool age) child, attention and praise themselves may be sufficient to establish standards and make her feel good about performance. That is, provided the child is treated by others in positive ways and told she is loved and valued, she may feel good about herself. With age, however, what children consider rewarding may change. The school-age child may find it more important to get the right answer—to perform successfully, for instance, on the baseball field or in the classroom—than to be praised for trying hard. Along with this change comes children's increasing awareness of and concern with the social world. This is reflected in an increasing tendency for children to evaluate themselves *in comparison to* others. Thus, what is important is not so much praise or even success, but whether a child performs as well as, for instance, his peers do on any given task. The transition to adolescence brings with it still other changes. As we noted in chapter 3, this is a time when the youngster becomes increasingly introspective. His concern with his own thought is associated with a new form of egocentrism. That is, the young teen may imagine that everyone else is concentrating as much attention on him as he himself is. Elkind (1978) refers to this phenomenon as the teenager's "imaginary audience." As such, the young adolescent may be overly sensitive about others' potential reactions to him, and stringent standards set during this time may reflect his concerns with others' evaluations of his performance.

It is important to note that this sequence—from a focus on social reinforcement to successful performance to social comparison to the concern with an imaginary audience—is not timed absolutely to specific ages. Nor does one basis for establishing standards always precede or follow another in every area of endeavor. Finally, a youngster's feelings about himself may be based on several of these sources of standards. For instance, a child may feel good about his academic abilities both because he gets As, *and* because he does better in school than do his siblings. The point is that standards come from different sources; that these sources change to a certain degree during development; and that, in intervention, it is important to develop a sense of why a child holds a particular set of standards.

In summary, children (and adults) with low self-esteem often have adopted very high, almost unattainable standards. When standards are unrealistically high, a child will frequently experience failure and seldom experience success. To help a child gain a more positive self-evaluation, his standards must be examined and revised.

Children who have difficulty being introspective about their thoughts and feelings will at first find it hard to use the interventions described in this chapter. Using several concrete examples, such as the ones provided, may be helpful. Keep in mind the developmental course of private speech, discussed in chapter 6, which applies to standard setting also.

When helping a child to modify his standards for success and failure, it is important to provide guidance about what may be realistically attainable. However, a teacher or counselor must take care not to impose his own standards onto the child in this process.

ASSESSMENT OF CHILDREN'S STANDARDS

When attempting to examine and modify a child's standards, assessment and treatment blend together, since a major goal of the intervention is to help a child assess his own patterns of standard setting.

The purposes of this assessment are to examine the child's perceptions of success and failure in her life and to determine if her expectations for herself are realistic. Begain by explaining that the topics for this session include the goals we set for ourselves (and that other people set for us) and the way they affect our feelings about ourselves. Ask the child to give some examples of times she has been successful and times she has failed. How did she know these were successes and failures (did other people tell her, did she know because of her feelings, etc.)? Who sets her goals—parents, teachers, herself? What happens if her expectations for herself are not met? Does she make any negative self-statements when she does not meet her expectations? To what extent does she feel that her goals and standards can be moved to be more or less strict than they are? This should be set up as a comfortable discussion, with questions asked in an accepting manner. The goal is to help the child start thinking about these issues. Using concrete examples supplied by the child will help younger children to be able to think about these rather abstract matters.

For example, a child might describe striking out in a baseball game as a recent failure. He felt it was a failure because of his own disappointment and because his teammates were displeased. His parents watched the game and were not upset with his strikeout, so he thought his standards about his performance in baseball games might come from his coach, teammates, and himself. When he strikes out, he said he feels "disappointed" with himself and "sad." He thought he might be making a self-statement such as "I'm a terrible baseball player." He felt he might be able to revise this standard to be less critical, because it did seem unreasonable to expect to never strike out; after all, major league players strike out and they are certainly not "terrible baseball players."

As an exercise, ask the child to list three or four areas that are fairly important to her in which she can experience success and failure. Some examples are school grades, sports, friends, playing a musical instrument, and hobbies. Work separately on each area. Ask the child for concrete standards of success and failure. The child probably has not thought about this sort of discrete cutting point between success and failure, so she may have some trouble with it at first. School grades are a good place to start, since grades are very concrete. For example, she may tell you that she considers an A or B a success, and a D or F a failure. Inquire about a "middle ground" which is considered neither success nor failure. In this example, a C would probably be placed in the middle. When limits for success, failure and middle ground are established, find out how often she falls into each category. Perhaps she gets As and Bs 75% of the time, Cs about 20%, and Ds and Fs about 5% of the time. Next, find out about the feelings associated with each category. Try to get her to be specific about her feelings; if she says she feels "bad" when she fails, ask if she feels "disappointed" or "angry with herself" (this area will be addressed in detail in chapter 10, under the topic of Differential Affect Training).

Here are some examples of the kind of information that should be elicited. One boy listed "other kids teasing me" as an important area for him. He considered it a successful day when he was teased only two or three times; this happened once or twice a week, and he felt very happy and relieved on those days. Failure was being teased nine to ten times or more during a school day. He felt mad all day when this happened, usually only once every two weeks. Middle ground, in between success and failure (being teased four to eight times a day), made him feel sad at the time of the teasing, but not at other times. These days occurred three or four times each week.

This boy also listed "friends" as an area of importance. Being successful with friends was defined as having at least one very good friend. He felt it would be a failure for him if he had no good friends, even if he had some acquaintances. There was no middle ground here. Since he presently had three or four good friends, he felt successful and satisfied in this area. He said that he has never been without at least one good friend.

After all areas the child has listed have been worked out in this manner, look to see what the information tells you about her. How often does she experience success and failure? How good does she feel with successes, and how bad does she feel with failures? Discuss with her the importance of setting goals that are appropriate for what she is able to do. It is important to be able to experience success sometimes, and to minimize the amount of failure experienced. Has the child set such narrow criteria for success that it is seldom achieved? Explain the importance of having a middle ground as a "buffer area." Perhaps the child wishes to maintain fairly stringent criteria for success; a wide middle ground, into which her efforts fall much of the time, can protect her from failure. In other words, even when something is less than an absolute success, it need not be regarded as an abject failure. Instead, it can be placed into a more neutral area, preventing the child from experiencing more failure than is necessary. Another way of avoiding large amounts of failure is to set a fairly low standard of success. In the "friends" example above, the child was satisfied with only one very good friend, and he had always been able to meet that goal. Consequently, he never experienced failure.

Talk with the child about any of her standards that appear to be misplaced, particularly those which result in frequent failure. See if she feels that any of the criteria for success and failure could be adjusted. Try to help her make room for a generous middle ground.

Throughout the assessment, when you discover a troublesome area, you will want to attempt to identify the specific location of the problem so that it can be targeted for intervention:

Is the standard reasonable, but the child fails frequently due to lack of skills? Remediation of skills is not addressed in this chapter; however, communication skills, aimed at enhancing social relations, are discussed in chapter 11. Poor academic skills should be evaluated to determine whether some type of special assistance could be applied, if this has not already been done. In many other areas—athletic ability/skill at sports, physical attractiveness, musical or artistic talent—there is a wide variability in "normal" ability, and the child's standards must reflect a realistic understanding of her own limitations. This is not to suggest, however, that she should stop practicing or striving to improve where it is feasible.

Is the standard itself unrealistic? Sometimes very gifted children will consider a single mistake to be a failure; their exceptional abilities seem to somehow justify a belief that if they tried hard enough, they could be perfect. Alternatively, parents who value achievement can instill unrealistically high expectations in a child. Depending on the child's age, she could be comparing herself unfavorably with her classmates, or she may feel "on stage," thus magnifying the impact of a less-than-ideal performance. Try to determine the source of the unrealistic standard.

How does the child interpret a success or a failure? Perhaps the child's standard is reasonable, and her skill level enables her to attain success fairly often. Her attributions will play an important role in how she feels about success and failure. For instance, if she makes a specific, external, or unstable attribution for a success ("I was just lucky this time"), she will be reducing the potential positive impact upon her self-esteem. Similarly, if she makes a global, internal, or stable attribution to a failure ("I'm a terrible artist— my projects never turn out right"), she will be magnifying the effect of a single negative incident, resulting in a heavy blow to her self-esteem. Self-statements can work in the same way to deflate the positive effect ("My report was good, but it's nothing compared to Joan's") or inflate the negative effect ("Everyone saw me strike out—they must think I'm a total klutz!") of an incident.

Remind the child what she has learned about self-statements and attributions, and ask her to help you to assess her use of these cognitive strategies in the area of standard setting. Also, refer if necessary to the section of chapter 5 which introduces Basic Feeling Identification, because feelings are often the cue for the types of attributions or self-statements that are used.

INTERVENTIONS

Standard Setting: Basic Model

The assessment will have laid the groundwork for use of the basic model. Now, present the steps involved in examining and modifying standards:

1. Think of an area where you experience success and failure.
2. Make concrete, explicit statements about what equals a success and what equals a failure. Is there a middle ground (a level of performance that is neither success nor failure)?
3. How often does your performance fall into the category of success? failure? middle ground? What feelings do you have when you experience each of these categories?
4. Decide if you are feeling like you have failed more than you need to (are you feeling bad about yourself too often?). If not, your standards are probably comfortable for you. If so, continue with the next step.

5. Think about ways you could modify your standards. You could change your standard for success, so you can feel good more often. Or you could lower your standard for failure, and make your middle ground (the place where you feel OK, but not like a success or a failure) larger. You could do both.
6. Examine the attributions and self-statements you use after performances which fall into success, middle ground, or failure categories. Your thoughts should be helping you to feel good about success, neutral about middle ground, and disappointed (but not destroyed) about failure.

Encourage the child to use self-critical thoughts (negative self-statements and attributions) and feelings as a cue for using these steps to examine and modify her standards. The perspective of an adult she trusts may be helpful in deciding how to revise her standards.

Continue (or review) the work begun in the assessment phase until you and the child have worked through the standards she has established in all major areas of her life. Keep a list of these standards for future use.

Modification of Standards

In the last exercise, the child's own standards for himself were identified and perhaps modified. This exercise will explore the effect of others on the child's standards. For each area in which he has a standard, ask him to talk about the standards others have for him. Identify success, middle ground, and failure, as set up by (a) parents, (b) teachers, and (c) peers. There may be other significant people who should be included as well, such as siblings, a coach, grandparents, or an employer. Now compare the lists. Whose standards most closely match the child's? Whose are more discrepant? If there are large disparities between different people, this could indicate a source of conflict for the child. For example, remaining true to parental standards could result in ostracism by peers, while endorsing peers' values could lead to family friction. Youngsters of different ages will approach this problem differently, as was described earlier in this chapter, with younger children relying more on adult approval and older children comparing themselves to peers. Discuss the difficulties inherent in the process of establishing one's own standards, and explore the child's comfort with making changes in this area. Some children may feel the need to be rigid about their standards, feeling parental disapproval or peer rejection will result. If this is the case, rather than insist on the child changing a standard "for his own good," simply observe the effect this standard has on his feelings for himself.

Perhaps at another time he will feel more able to be flexible. If the child does uncover an area in which he wishes to change, work through the process using the steps described above for modifying standards.

Modifying Attributions and Self-Statements
Related to Standards

Once you and the child have a clear understanding of the way his standards operate in his life, and you have worked together to modify some of his troublesome standards, you can now turn your attention to the child's cognitive responses to success and failure. As mentioned in the Basic Model, the goal is for the child to feel positive about successes, neutral about middle-ground experiences, and somewhat (but not overwhelmingly) negative about failures. Explore the child's use of attributions and self-statements. To do this, it may be helpful to have him recall specific instances when his performance fell into success, middle ground, and failure categories, and then remember the feeling he had with each of these. Were his feelings in line with what you would expect, or were they less positive than they should be? If the child is unable to remember any of these situations, he can try to imagine situations, as realistically as possible, where his performance falls into each of the three categories, and then imagine how he would feel. Imagining is a less effective way to do this, however, since it may not accurately reflect the child's "real world." The homework may also be used as an opportunity for the child to monitor his attributions and self-statements, and then bring back for discussion any cognitions that were problematic for him. Once any difficulties with attributions or self-statements are discovered, work with the child to change them, using the procedures outlined in chapters 6 and 7.

Be aware that these cognitive interpretations of performance may vary across different situations. For example, a young child who experiences a success by her standards may be able to feel proud—unless a significant adult, such as a parent or teacher, responds, "You could have done better than that." Or a child who experiences a success may discount it when his friends' performances are better, but accept it when his own performance surpasses theirs. Both developmental and individual (specific to the child) differences will affect this type of cross-situational instability.

HOMEWORK

Use of homework is essential when attempting to help a child modify his standards. First, it will be important for him to monitor his own responses to his performance after he has been made aware of these issues, because he will undoubtedly uncover some surprising new information that is different from what he initially discussed with you. Monitoring will also be necessary on an ongoing basis, so that he can detect signs indicating a need to change a cognitive process (i.e., the standard itself, or the related attributions and self-statements). Second, the child will need to practice using his new standards, attributions, and self-statements, and can then use the next session to discuss any difficulties he had and to work out the rough spots. For some children, it is surprising how quickly the exercise of specifying success and failure standards can affect their feelings about their experiences.

When assigning homework, ask him to be aware of successes and failures in the areas you have discussed together. He should try to notice the feelings he experiences, and check to see if these correspond to the criteria for success and failure he has set with you—is he feeling good about successes and neutral about falling into the middle ground, or is he regarding the middle ground as failure and feeling bad about those experiences? Ask him to try to remember—or better yet, write down— the details of any situations involving standards. You will want to discuss thee performance itself, how it measured up to the standard, the cognitive interpretation, and the subsequent feelings associated with the event. Also explore the role of other people in the situation—did they affect his feelings about how well he did? Ideally, the child should repeat several times this homework exercise of observing himself and then reporting back, with several days or a week in between each session.

Chapter 10

Social Understanding and Skills

Social understanding and social cognition are terms used to describe a person's comprehension of another's point of view. The ability to take another's perspective is one that develops dramatically during the school age years. It involves understanding others' thoughts, feelings and ways of experiencing the physical world, as well as their personal characteristics (Livesley & Bromley, 1973; Shantz, 1983).

Children's level of social understanding is important to their self-esteem in two ways. First, as we noted in chapter 3, children derive their ideas about who they are (that is, their self-concepts), at least in part, from the way others see them (Mead, 1934). Being able to gauge accurately *how* another sees the self, and *why* one is perceived that way, is consequently an integral part of self-knowledge. Social understanding may also have an impact on how a child evaluates himself because a child with better social understanding may be better able to treat others in ways they like (Asher, 1978). In turn, this may make others respond positively to the child, and make him feel good about himself.

In this chapter we outline strategies for promoting social understanding in children. After elaborating on our definition of social cognition by identifying its different components, we discuss the developmental course of social cognition, what causes its growth, and the significance of social understanding for children's well-being. Given that we will be describing four different components of children's social understanding, the assessment and treatment section of this chapter is longer than usual and will be divided into four sections reflecting each of these components. We then review assessment strategies for determining a child's level of abilities, and finally we outline our program for helping children to develop their abilities to understand others.

THE DEVELOPMENT OF SOCIAL UNDERSTANDING

Children's understanding of others involves a number of abilities, each of which may develop at different rates. These abilities include children's understanding of others' thoughts, emotions and perceptions (Shantz, 1975) and their knowledge of what another is like. A preschooler, for example, may understand that "Daddy is upset," even though she cannot possibly grasp the thoughts which distress her father. In this way her *emotional perspective taking* skills are limited. In some situations, preschoolers may show an appreciation for anothers' perceptual experiences (of the physical world), as when they raise their voices to communicate from a distance or when, in showing someone a picture they have drawn, they turn it around to face the other person. But a young child's *perceptual perspective taking* skills fail him in some situations—a fact appreciated by adults who have had the experience of talking on the telephone with a preschooler who has answered their questions with a nod or shake of the head rather than a spoken "yes" or "no." Finally, even a young child can tell you what her best friend is like; her *description of another's characteristics* ("Joanie has brown hair and a cabbage patch doll"), however, will be very different from that of a school age child or adolescent ("Joanie is intelligent and sensitive; I can always count on her").

In our discussion of treatment goals and strategies, we focus on four areas of social cognition: (a) what another sees or hears (that is, the other person's *perceptual* experiences); (b) what another *thinks* (including what he knows and what his intentions are); (c) what another *feels*; and (d) what another *is like*.

As children mature in each of these four areas, they develop from an *egocentric* perspective on the world to an increasingly more accurate comprehension about just what the different perspective of another person might be. An egocentric child acts as if others' perspectives are the same as his own; as such, a preschooler, for instance, may select a matchbox car for his father's birthday present because he thinks this is just what Dad would want. The school age child may know that others' points of view are different, but still may have trouble accurately judging them. Consequently, when shopping for father's birthday, she may choose a present that is appropriate for an adult, such as a tie, but one that is not suitable for Dad on account of its color, pattern, or style. By adolescence, however, a youngster is likely to have an accurate idea about what another's point of view is: he will know what Dad would like for his birthday, and he also will know that if he is unsure about his cloice, he should consult with someone else.

[margin note: Age 7 6-7 perspective taking]

[left margin note: Repression — focus moves from Consequences of act to focus on intention of act. an intent or act]

Before the age of about six or seven years many children do not seem to have much of an interest in others' different perspectives on the world. If asked, preschoolers may be able to tell you how someone else feels or what he thinks (for instance, "he was just pretending"; "it was an accident"), but still they seem to have little interest in figuring out the connection between another's perspective on the world and that person's behavior. A good example of children's developing concern with this connection between another's perspective and behavior is the development of lying; when children lie, they may deliberately try to control the perspective of another, such as a parent ("*I* didn't break that cup, the dog must have knocked it off the table!"), in an effort to control that person's behavior (for instance, punishment). Early on, children's lies tend to be flimsy and unconvincing; adults should take heart in realizing that the clever lies of older youngsters are examples of their developing social and cognitive abilities!

In the realm of moral judgment, young children's understanding of right and wrong during the egocentric period tends to be focused on the good or bad consequences of an act rather than on the *intention* of the act (Kohlberg, 1969; Piaget, 1932). Thus, at this developmental level a boy who breaks two plates while helping do the dishes may be judged more negatively than a boy who only breaks one plate while climbing up to a cabinet to take a forbidden cookie.

Finally, children's understanding, during the preschool and early school age period, of what others are like is limited to concrete attributes (brown-haired, skinny) or possessions. As such, the development of concepts of others parallels the development of the self-concept as we described in chapter 3 (Livesley & Bromley, 1973). Table 10.1 shows the progression of changes that take place in children's social knowledge during the school-age years and beyond. It is important to note that the age ranges described here are very general guidelines. A child may show a great deal of variability in his level of performance depending upon the complexity of the task. Tasks with concrete referents presented in simple language in which the child can respond nonverbally may allow the child to show a more advanced level of skill.

TABLE 10.1. Developmental Changes in Role Taking, Behavior Evaluations and Conceptions of Personal Characteristics of Self and Others[1]

Role Taking	Behavior Evaluations	Person Perception
Stage 1—Egocentric Viewpoint (3–6 years)	Premoral	Concrete and Absolute Conceptions
1) Knows that self and other perspectives differ	1) Evaluations based on good vs. bad consequences—not intentions	1) Describes self and other according to physical attributes or possessions
2) Can label or describe		2) Sees characteristics as

others' thoughts, feelings, or perceptual experience if asked 3) Often fails to distinguish between own and others' perspectives in day-to-day behavior 4) Fails to see connection between others' points of view and their behavior.	2) Evaluations based on consequences to the self (for instance, "It's bad if I get caught and punished") 3) Reasons for evaluations simply assert but do not justify decision about what is right or wrong.	either/or attributes 3) Believes concrete characteristics are fundamental to the persistence of a person's identity (thus, if a child grew his hair and wore dresses he would no longer be a boy).
Stage 2— Social–Informational Role-Taking (age 6–8 years) 1) Knows that others' perspectives are different and based on others' reasoning and experiences 2) Can only focus on one (self or other) perspective at a time.	Punishment and Obediance Orientation 1) Focuses on one perspective—that of authority or powerful figures 2) Understands that good actions are based on good intentions 3) Beginning sense of fairness.	Interpersonal and Concrete Conceptions 1) Beginning an orientation to interpersonal attributes of self and other 2) Attributes still are absolute 3) Attributes of others may be limited to those displayed interactions with the child herself.
Stage 3—Self-Reflective Role Taking (8–10 years) 1) Aware that each person is aware of others' perspectives 2) Knows that awareness affects one's view of self and other 3) Knows that an understanding of others can be gained by putting oneself in another's situation 4) Cannot see own and others' perspective simultaneously.	Instrumental Orientation 1) Moral reciprocity is basis of evaluations of behavior ("if someone is mean to me it is all right to be mean to them".)	Interpersonal Conceptions 1) Increased and elaborated orientation to interpersonal characteristics 2) Beginning awareness that different situations demand different behaviors 3) Beginning awareness that others may have many motives for a behavior and that these motives may be conflicting, and that motives may be ordered in terms of importance.
Stage 4—Mutual Role Taking (10–12 years) 1) Can distinguish views of participants in an interaction or relationship from the perspective of an outsider 2) Realizes that each person can view the	Orientation to Maintaining Mutual Expectations 1) Right is defined as the Golden Rule 2) Child considers all points of view including each person's motives as a basis for evaluations of an action.	Interpersonal Conceptions 1) Child begins to see consistency over time as basis for person's identity 2) Evaluation of interpersonal characteristics based not only on immediate consequences to self, but on general and long term

self, other and their relationship from an objective (third person) point of view 3) Knows that each person can put herself in the other's position before deciding how to behave (the Golden Rule).		effects as well as on behavior toward others besides the self.
Stage 5—Social and Conventional System Role-Taking (12–15+ years) 1) Realizes that mutual perspective-taking does not always lead to complete understanding 2) Sees social conventions as valuable because they are understood by everyone.	Orientation to Society's Perspective 1) Right is defined as the majority perspective 2) Behaviors are judged on the basis of their consequences for society—not individuals 3) Emphasis on maintaining social order.	Conceptions of Others' Attitudes, Beliefs and Values 1) Differentiated conception of interpersonal characteristics 2) Orientation to others' attitudes, values and beliefs, which tend to be seen in absolute terms.

[1] First two columns adapted from "Social–Cognitive Understanding: A Guide to Educational and Clinical Practice," by R. Selman, in Moral Development and Behavior, T. Lickona, Ed. Copyright 1976, Holt, Rinehart, & Winston.

The first column in Table 10.1 shows the progression of children's role-taking abilities. In this realm we see that children become increasingly able to use, in their social behavior and relationships with others, their understanding that: (a) another person will have a different perspective, and (b) they can learn what that perspective might be.

In terms of their understanding of the morality of their own and other's behavior (Column 2), children become increasingly oriented to people's *intentions* as opposed to the objective or concrete consequences of their behavior. In addition, they move from an absolutist position (something is either right or wrong) to a more *differentiated and relativistic* understanding—for instance, that the same behavior may be evaluated differently depending on the situation (Kohlberg, 1969; Piaget, 1932). Thus, a child may evaluate himself negatively when he does something to cause his peers to reject him *if* his behavior has harmed someone else or if it was intentionally mean. The child may feel proud of himself for the same behavior, however, if his intentions were good or if he believes the long-term consequences may be beneficial. For instance, one youngster's self-esteem may be hurt by the rejection of peers or siblings who are angry that he "tattled" on them because of their smoking or drinking. In contrast, another youngster may be able to convince himself that his behavior was directed at preserving the health and well-being of his friends.

The third aspect of developmental change in this area pertains to youngster's ideas about what people (themselves and others) are like (Column 3 in Table 10.1). As we noted in chapter 3, these conceptions change from a concern with *concrete* and physical characteristics (what I look like, what I have) to *interpersonal* characteristics (how I treat others) to ideas about a person's *values, beliefs* or *attitudes*, which emerge in the mid- to late adolescent years. From the preschool to adolescent years, conceptions of self and other also become less absolute and more *differentiated* (Livesley & Bromley, 1973).

Influences on the Development of Social Understanding

Developmental changes in children's social understanding, as well as differences in social understanding between children of the same age, seem to be caused by both cognitive abilities and social experiences with their parents and their friends. As children move from the preschool years to adolescence, the way they think seems to change drastically. The preschooler's thinking, for instance, has been labeled "intuitive," because her ideas seem to be tied to her own idiosyncratic experiences. Consequently, a child is likely to say that the reasons behind another's feelings of sadness are those that usually are linked to the child's own feelings of sadness: Daddy looks sad when he comes home from work because he is sick or because he does not like what is being prepared for dinner.

At school age, sometimes called the *concrete operational* period of cognitive development, children are capable of logical thinking, but their thoughts are tied to observable situations. At this age, for instance, the child understands that causes precede effects, and thus she may reason that something happened at work to make her father look sad. At this age, however, the child may have little understanding about what events at work would have such an effect, or if she does make some guesses, they will be tied to what little she knows about work (for example, "Daddy got fired," or "Daddy's boss got mad at him"). By adolescence, many youngsters are capable of abstract and hypothetical reasoning— sometimes called *formal operational* thought. At this age, youngsters can imagine events and situations outside of their own experiences and, therefore, may more accurately understand another person's perspective (Flavell, 1985).

One way that children develop their social understanding abilities is by having experiences with others who have different perspectives from their own. Friends who are about a child's own age are particularly important in this respect; though their ideas may be different (for example, slightly more advanced than a child's own ideas), they still may be similar enough for the child to understand. This idea—that examples of different thinking styles should be *optimally discrepant* from a child's own level of ability in order to promote development—is one that will be important in our treatment considerations.

Parents also help to develop social understanding by modeling a concern for others' points of view and welfare, especially in their discipline strategies. Several research studies have shown that parents who set clear and consistent limits for their children's behavior, and who provide reasons for their rules and for rewards and punishments, have children whose social understanding is advanced relative to that of their agemates (Maccoby & Martin, 1983). A child whose parents listen to the reasons she has for her behavior and may sometimes alter the rules depending on the persuasiveness of that child's arguments, also tends to show more advanced social understanding abilities. These abilities, in turn, seem to be related to children's popularity with and acceptance by peers, to their altruistic behavior and feelings of empathy toward others, and to their emotional stability. Problems in comprehending others' points of view, on the other hand, are related to behavior problems such as impulsivity and aggression (Dodge & Frame, 1982).

Given the dramatic changes in children's social understanding during the school-age years and the possibility of large differences between the abilities of children of the same age, it is important to accurately assess a child's level of social understanding in order to determine the direction of intervention. Additionally, because children's abilities in the areas of understanding—perceptual perspective taking, understanding what another thinks, knowing how another feels, and comprehending what another is like—all develop at different rates, each of these abilities must be assessed separately. In the following pages we outline techniques for measuring and treating children's competencies.

PERCEPTUAL PERSPECTIVE TAKING

Assessment

Perceptual perspective taking, for most children, is the simplest kind of social understanding. The basic tasks can be made more or less complex, depending upon the age of the child. For younger school-age children (ages 7–8 years) it will be important to find out whether they actually *can* determine, for instance, how a scene will be viewed from another position. For older youngsters, you will want to determine whether they actually *use* what they know in interpersonal situations. Use Table 10.1 (Column 1) to evaluate children's performances.

Three Figures Task. For this procedure you will need three to five objects of different shapes (such as blocks) and drawing materials (pencil or crayon and paper). You and the child should be seated initially at opposite sides of a small table.

Tell the child that the purpose of the game is to see how well she can figure out what you see. Place three objects in the center of the table and then tell the child to draw a picture of what *you* see in front of you. The child's picture should be a mirror image of her own perceptual experience.

You can make this task more difficult by using more objects, by using objects of the same shape but different colors, or by making the layout of the objects more complicated (for instance, placing the object in a straight line is an easier task, a triangular figure with objects equidistant from one another is a slightly more complicated task, and a figure in which distance between objects varies is even more difficult).

Repeat this task, this time seated at a right angle to the child.

In addition to asking the child to *draw* your perspective, you also should question the child about the difference between your perspectives. For instance, when the child is seated opposite you, she should be able to say that your view is the opposite of her own view.

Show me/Tell me Task. For this task you will need drawing paper, pencils and crayons, and a picture book.

This procedure is designed to reveal whether the child naturally takes another's perceptual perspective into account during social interactions. To begin, you and the child again should be seated at opposite sides of a table. Later, you should move to sit at right angles to the child in an effort to determine how much the child's behavior changes as a result of where you are seated.

Have the child draw a picture, and when it is completed ask her to show you the picture. Determine how much the child moves the picture to accommodate your view. If she fails to hold up the picture to face you or to turn the picture around on the table, tell the child that you cannot see the picture very well and determine whether this feedback is followed by the child's changing the orientation of the picture.

Similar information can be obtained by asking the child to tell a story based on a picture book. Determine whether the child alters the orientation of the book to accommodate to your position. At some time during this story you should interrupt the child, saying, 'Excuse me?" or "What?" Determine whether the child alters her articulation or increases the loudness of her voice as a consequence. If not say, "I'm sorry, I can't hear you/understand you," and determine whether this feedback results in altered behavior.

Guessing Game. You and the child should be seated at opposite sides of the table. Look at different objects in the room (including parts of the child's own body or clothing) and ask the child to "Guess what I'm looking at." Repeat this game using more subtle orientation cues until you are sure the child is capable of "reading" your behavior.

Intervention

The most appropriate tasks for helping children in this area are those described in the assessment section.

Three Figures Task. This activity can be elaborated by choosing different kinds of figures and by asking the child to describe the perspective of a puppet or a doll instead of that of the examiner (that is, holding the puppet in different locations and asking what the puppet sees). Children may respond verbally (while you make a drawing of what the child says, so that this can be compared later with the puppet's actual perspective). Children also may be given an alternative set of materials to arrange, they may draw a picture of the other's perspective, or they may be asked to choose from a set of photographs, the one that matches the puppet's (or other's) perspective. The child should be given feedback about his answers by having him compare his responses to the puppet's response (that is, by asking him to move to the same side of the table as the puppet).

Show me/Tell me Task. This activity should be conducted this time with feedback to the child about his behavior. For instance, the examiner may say, "I'm sorry I can't see that picture very well. Please turn it around so it faces me." This task can be used casually in general social exchanges with the child. For instance, you may ask the child to show you his new sneakers and then provide feedback about how well the child has adapted to your visual perspective; "Those new sneakers are pretty jazzy. Thank you for holding your foot out so that I could see them really well." Similarly, when necessary, you may give the child feedback about your auditory perspectives: "I'm sorry, I can't hear you. Would you speak more loudly/clearly?;" "When you talk so loudly it hurts my ears. Would you lower your voice a little?"

Guessing Game. In this activity one person looks toward an object and the other guesses what she is looking at. This game can be elaborated by having each of you take turns at each role, and it can be made more complicated by each player looking at a series of objects and having the other guess the whole series. (Some children may change their minds about what they have looked at after you make your guess. It may be useful to have the child write down the items he has looked at so that you cannot be "fooled" in this way!) When playing this game, you may provide information about how you know what the child is looking at to model appropriate behavior in this situation: "I saw you looking over my shoulder and checked to see what you might be looking at. It was either the door or the coat rack, so I had to look at your eyes more closely to see in what direction they were looking."

As mentioned, perceptual perspective taking is the simplest of the social understanding abilities, and simple forms of these tasks should be mastered by second or third graders. Some children may have special problems with insensitivity to or ignorance of another's perceptual experiences—especially experiences that are tied to particularly emotional states. For instance, a child may be especially loud, not realizing how his noisiness is perceived (and responded to emotionally) by others. A child also may be physically rough partly because he does not know that such physical contact is perceived as painful by others (and that, in turn, it gives rise to negative emotions such as anger, fear, or sadness). A child also may fail to understand that people have different tolerances for physical sensation—or that the same person can experience the same event (tickling, loud noise) differently at different times (when she is tired, when she is sick). Because these aversive or potentially pleasant sensations tend to be linked to emotional expressions, we discuss relevant intervention strategies in the section on emotional perspective-taking. This link between perceptual perspective taking and other kinds of perspective taking, however, should be recognized, as both forms of social understanding may underlie problem behavior.

EMOTIONAL PERSPECTIVE TAKING

Assessment

Although some of these tasks can be difficult, most children should have a relatively easy time on simple feeling-identification tasks. The four basic emotions we deal with here are happiness, sadness, anger, and fear. In the case of older youngsters, additional emotions (for instance, proud, excited, disgusted) also may be added to the exercises. Use Table 10.1 (Column 1) to evaluate children's responses.

Feeling Identification I: Faces. For this procedure you can use either photographs or books that picture people displaying the four basic emotions (happiness, sadness, anger, and fear). Begin by using pictures of children who are about the same age and of the same sex as the child. You can move on to pictures of adults or pictures of members of the opposite sex at a later point. For each picture ask the child how the person in the picture feels.

Next ask the child to "make faces" that convey each of the four basic emotions. Finally, you should "make faces," and ask the child to describe how you feel. Begin by using more exaggerated expressions and once the child shows her capabilities, use more subtle means of conveying different emotions.

Feeling Identification II: Stories. For this procedure you will need a set of brief stories. For younger children, these should be accompanied by pictures, in order to keep the child interested. After each story the child should be questioned about how the character(s) feel. The stories should be graded in difficulty as follows:

1. A single character, the same age and sex as the child. Something happens or the character behaves in a manner that produces a single emotion.
   For example: After practicing every afternoon for weeks, Jill wins first place in a running race at school.
2. A single adult character in a situation that produces a single emotion.
   For example: A man winding his watch drops and breaks it.
3. Multiple characters whose activities produce similar emotions.
   For example: Jill wins a running race at school and her parents are there to watch her (ask how each person feels).
4. Multiple characters whose activities produce *discrepant* emotions.
   For example: Jill and Beth both have practiced for the big race. On the day of the race Beth is sick and cannot come to school. Jill wins the race.
5. A single character whose activities produce mixed feelings.
   For example: Jill runs in the race and makes first place, but her best friend Beth loses another race that she runs.
   Or:
   Jill runs in the race and makes second place; her best friend Beth makes first place.
   For the above examples of mixed feelings, determine the child's understanding of *each* character's emotions.
6. Construct a story in which the character's intentions and the outcome of her behavior are first similar, then discrepant, to determine on which dimension the child focuses in evaluating the character's feelings.
   For example: Jill wants to win the race but another girl is running right beside her as they come to the finish line. Jill pushes against the other girl and makes it look like an accident so no one else can tell, but the other girl does not slow down at all. At the finish line, Jill just barely wins the race.

Versus:
Jill wants to win the race but another girl is right next to her. Jill knows she has to run even faster. As she speeds up she accidentally bumps into the other girl who trips and falls. Jill wins the race.

In these stories, more mature children will probably make a distinction between the feelings of a character with good intentions whose actions have negative consequences and a character with bad intentions whose actions do not have negative consequences. More mature children will focus on *intentions*, less mature children on the *consequences* of a behavior, as can be seen in Table 10.1, Column 2.

Feeling Identification III: Discrepant Cues. For this procedure you will need brief stories and pictures of characters displaying each of the four basic emotions. These stories should be paired with a picture displaying a character whose emotion does not match the emotion that *should* be experienced by the character in the story. For example, a story of Jill winning a race might be accompanied by a picture of a girl looking afraid. First, ask the child how the character feels. More mature children will focus on the story content rather than the picture, or, at minimum, point out the discrepancy between the two.

Intervention

Again, many activities for teaching understanding of others' emotions or feelings can be adapted from the assessment tasks. Additionally, some of the tasks described in the previous section on cognitive perspective-taking can be expanded to include practice in recognizing one's own and others' feelings (for instance, role-playing and discussions of books and movies).

Differential Affect Training. Before you begin actual identification of expressed feelings, it is important to teach the youngster to label the feeling dimensions. Furthermore, the child should learn labels for intensity of feelings along each of the dimensions. This process, called *Differential Affect Training* (Craighead, Moyers, & Craighead, 1986), teaches the child labels for degrees of feeling on a number of basic dimensions. For our purposes here we will use the bipolar dimension of happy––sad, the unipolar dimension of neutral–anger, and the bipolar dimension of fear– brave. Other dimensions, such as love–hate, anxious––relaxed, and surprise–bored, may be useful with older children.

As an exercise, give the child a stack of index cards, each of which has a feeling word from Table 10.2 typed on it. Ask the youngster to sort the cards into categories relevant to each of the dimensions, e.g., a stack of happy–sad words, a stack of brave–scared words, and a stack of neutral–angry words. The child should use as many of the words as possible, putting aside those words for which he does not know the meaning.

TABLE 10.2. Personal Attributes

affectionate	good
afraid	happy
aggravated	hopeless
aggressive	hostile
amused	impatient
angry	irritated
annoyed	jealous
bashful	joyful
blue	lonely
bored	loving
brave	mad
calm	miserable
cheerful	nervous
contented	outraged
cool	panicky
cross	peaceful
daring	pleasant
delighted	rage
depressed	reckless
disagreeable	rejected
discouraged	sad
disgusted	satisfied
displeased	scared
enraged	secure
enthusiastic	shaky
fearful	shy
fine	strong
forlorn	tense
friendly	terrible
frightened	terrified
frustrated	timid
furious	unhappy
gay	upset
glad	worried
gloomy	

After the words have been sorted into categories, ask the child to divide each group into these categories of intensity (strong, medium, and mild). Using these categories of intensity, ask the child now to rank order each feeling within each category, and write these words along a dimension line. For example, the neutral–angry dimension might be differentiated in the following way:

neutral   annoyed   irritated   frustrated   mad   angry   furious   rage

When working with the happy–sad dimension, some children, who focus heavily on negative feelings, put almost all the sad words into the strong intensity category. These same children may devalue the happy feelings by placing them in the mild intensity category. The result of this type of differentiation is a tendency to exaggerate any slightly bad feeling into intense sadness and a difficulty in feeling anything more positive than a mild or moderate happiness. This tendency can be partially overcome by the appropriate differentiation of labels for feeling states. You can use a rationale similar to standard setting (chapter 9) to teach the use of the entire dimensions; it does not have to be happy–sad since there are feelings between these endpoints. The goal is to teach appropriate labels for all the feelings, so the labels can be used to identify the child's own feelings and feelings in others.

Feeling Identification I: Faces. Explain to the child that

> Knowing how someone else is reacting to you should have an effect on what you do. For example, if you are talking to a friend and you can tell that she is getting bored, you might try to change the subject to something more interesting, or ask her a question, or suggest another activity. Sometimes it's hard to tell how another person is feeling. You have to depend not only on what she says, but on what she does. You might look at the expression on her face, and whether she is sitting calmly or nervously tapping her foot, for example. The exercise we're going to do today will give you practice in thinking about the way another person is feeling and thinking. Today we're going to practice guessing how the other one feels.

Take turns acting out different feelings, starting with the four basic emotions (happiness, sadness, anger, fear). Model your attention to relevant cues and give the child feedback about the way she conveys emotion. Ask her how she knows what you are feeling (that is, what cues she recognizes). You may want to start—especially with less sophisticated children—by exaggerating certain difficult-to-read cues. Let the child know that you are exaggerating these cues (and that it would be inappropriate to behave in such a manner in social interaction).

Feeling Identification II: Nonverbal Communication. Using the referential communication task, have the person in the "listener" role use only gestures and facial expressions to convey her understanding of the other's message (for instance, nods, frowns, smiles, pointing, etc.). It will be the "speaker's" job to decide if the "listener" understands her, and she must modify her actions accordingly. For this session, deliberately try to express a variety of responses—confusion, boredom, annoyance, satisfaction, and so forth—even if it is easy for you to complete the design, do so only if the child's instructions are clear enough and responsive enough to your expressions so that you truly could form the design if you were confused or bored or not paying attention. This time, try to be subtle and natural when expressing these responses: do not use exaggerated expressions. The point is to help the child become alert to the kinds of nonverbal expressions people naturally give in social interactions. After each design, stop and discuss the child's perception of your response. Tell her when she modified her actions in a helpful way and when she was not so helpful. If she is having difficulty reading your expressions, explain exactly what you were doing that expressed a particular emotion. When the child takes the "listener" role, give her feedback on the way she expressed her feelings.

Feeling Identification III: Stories. These stories should be constructed according to the graded levels of difficulty described in the section on assessment, with emphasis given to a child's area(s) of weakness. Ask the child to identify the emotion(s) experienced by the character or characters in a story and then discuss: (a) how the child knew the character would experience such an emotion; (b) the cause of the emotion; (c) any potential consequences of the emotion for the character or for others in the story. Be sure to have pictures or puppets to go along with the stories in the case of younger children.

Roleplay. If you can work with a child in a group, use the role playing exercise described earlier to discuss story characters' feelings, the causes of these emotions, and their consequences. As with thoughts and intentions, have children discuss the differences in their feelings as they assume the roles of different characters in the story. Be sure to help children recognize mixed emotions and to notice instances in which a character's observable behavior may not match his internal feelings (as when he is "hiding his emotions"). Discuss the reasons for mixed and hidden emotions and the possible consequences of these feelings for the individual and for those with whom he interacts.

Discussions of Books and Movies. This should be done in conjunction with discussions of story character's thoughts and intentions.

COGNITIVE PERSPECTIVE TAKING

Assessment

Comprehending what another knows or intends involves more sophisticated abilities than some of the previous tasks. Again, however, some abilities may be seen even in younger children.

Identifying What Another Knows. For this task, you will need to construct a set of stories, with pictures depicting incidents in the story (see example below). This task involves telling the child a story based on the entire set of pictured incidents. Then, after some of the picture incidents have been removed, the child is asked to describe the story his best friend would tell if he had not seen the missing pictures. The child is evaluated based on how much of the "privileged information" (from the pictures that are removed) infiltrates his friend's story.

Examples:

Picture 1: Henry is standing at the starting line, ready to run a race with two other boys.

Picture 2: The teacher says "go", and all the boys start to run.

Picture 3: Henry is far ahead of the other boys.

*Picture 4: A dog appears and chases Henry, snapping at his feet.

*Picture 5: Henry is frightened by the dog and stops; a man comes up and carries the dog away.

Picture 6: Henry wins the race.

Picture 7: The man comes up with his dog to tell Henry he is sorry that the dog chased him.

For this story, pictures #4 and #5 are removed and the child is asked to tell the story his friend would make up if his friend had never seen the missing pictures. Less mature children will mention something about Henry's fear of the dog and its cause. More mature children will recognize that their "friends" will have no information about such elements of the story.

Identifying What Another Thinks. For this task you will need a set of short stories. You also may use incidents from children's books. The task here is the same as that involved in identifying emotions. After the story or incident is read, the child is asked to describe what each character thinks. Ideally, stories should be written or chosen to maximize the discrepancies between the characters' points of view. The child should be asked what each character thinks about the incident that is portrayed. The examiner should be sensitive to the child's awareness of differences between the perspectives of different characters.

Referential Communication. For this exercise, you will need small blocks with different colored sides (for instance, the type used in the WISC–R for Block Design). Divide the blocks so that you and the child each have the same number of blocks of the same colors. You should sit facing each other at the small table and erect some sort of barrier between you so that you cannot see each other's blocks (an opened book stood on edge works well). Make up a variety of designs by placing the blocks in different patterns. Then form the first design with your blocks, being careful not to let the child see it. Your job now is to explain to the child how to form the identical design, without showing her your blocks or using any other type of visual information. When you have finished giving instructions and she feels she has completed the design, remove the barrier and compare your designs. (If they are the same, you have been successful.)

After the child understands the task, give her a set of designs and ask her to give you instructions on how to construct each pattern. Note the degree of egocentricity in the child's directions: for instance "Put this one right here," versus "Put a green block on the right side of a red block."

Guessing Game. For this task you will need two cups, a nickel, and a dime. Place a coin in each cup. Tell the child that his job is to guess which cup you will choose. If he guesses correctly, he gets the money in the cup you have chosen; if he guesses incorrectly, you get the money in the cup you have chosen. The actual choices in the game are unimportant. After the game is completed, however, no matter who wins, you should question the child about why he thought you would choose the cup you did. The youngest children may be unable to provide a rationale. Children who show some awareness of another's perspective will say they chose the dime because they thought you would want the larger amount of money. Children who understand the mutuality involved in perspective taking will give explanations that account for both perspectives ("You knew I'd guess you wanted the dime so you chose the nickel, instead:" "You knew I'd guess you'd try to fool me by choosing the nickel so you chose the dime," and so on).

Evaluating Others' Behaviors. For this task you will need a set of stories describing "moral dilemmas." After hearing each story, the child should be asked to evaluate the character's behavior and to provide the reasons behind her evaluations. The first kind of story involves a simple determination of whether the child's evaluations are based on *intentions* versus consequences of a character's behavior (Piaget, 1932). The second set are moral dilemmas in which the child is asked to explain why a behavior is right or wrong (Kohlberg, 1969).

Examples:

1. John wanted to surprise his parents by doing the dishes, but while he was putting them away, he broke one of the plates.
   Tim climbed up to get a cookie even though his parents had told him not to take any. He knocked over a plate on the shelf, but it didn't break. Which boy was more naughty?
     In this example, the child has to take into account differences between the boys' intentions *and* the consequences of their acts. For children who say that John was more naughty, simplify the task by concluding that both boys break a plate to determine whether this simplification makes a difference in whether the child will focus on intentions.

2. Heinz's wife is dying of a rare disease and only one kind of medicine can save her. One store sells the drug, but the man who owns the store is charging 100 times the real cost of the drug and Heinz can not afford it. Heinz has tried to borrow money, but no one will loan him any. Should Heinz steal the drug or should he let his wife die? Why?

You can use Table 10.1 (center column) to evaluate the level of the child's responses to moral dilemas. For instance, if a child's answer is that stealing is wrong or against the law, he would be at Stage 2 (punishment and obedience orientation). A child also might answer that the store owner is a mean and selfish man so it is all right to steal from him (Stage 3) or he might contrast Heinz's good intentions with the store owner's bad intentions or point out that anybody who needs medicine would want someone to get it for them (Stage 4).

Intervention

Again, the tasks used in assessment can be modified for treatment purposes, however give feedback this time about the child's performance, and let the child have the opportunity to switch roles with you.

Identifying Another's Perspective. If the child had problems in the first assessment activity, you can give him an abbreviated set of story cards first and ask him to construct a story; subsequently, the additional cards may be added and a second story developed. You should reinforce the difference in perspectives the child now has. For instance, in the story of Henry running a race, you may say: "You didn't know before what happened to Henry between the time he passed the other boys and the time he won the race. If you hadn't seen these two pictures you wouldn't know about that dog!" Practice with similar stories until the child begins to grasp these ideas about what others know.

Referential Communication. For the second activity, take turns being the giver and receiver of instructions. When you give instructions, model sensitivity to the child's responses ("You look confused—should I start over?" "You seem pretty confident—this must be easy for you;" "Looks like you're getting frustrated with this one;" "I think you're still thinking about this—shall I wait before I go on?"). When you receive instructions, try to use facial expression and other nonverbal as well as verbal responses to show your reactions to the child's messages.

Guessing Game. Using the format of the third assessment activity, use the cups with different coins (or different numbers of raisins or cereal pieces) in each and take turns being the one who guesses. When it is your turn to guess what the child's choice might be, model a reasoning strategy that is *one step above the child's own level* as determined in the assessment procedure. Thus, if the child guessed a cup at random or could not give a reason for his choice during assessment, say, "I'll bet you chose the cup with a dime because a dime is worth more than a nickel." If the child guessed you would choose the dime during the assessment activity say, "I first thought you'd choose the dime because it is worth more. Then I thought you'd know I'd guess the dime—so you would choose the nickel to fool me," (and so on). Certain children's games demand that each player be aware of the other's behavior—games like checkers or "Clue," for example—and these can be used to reinforce children's attention to what another may be thinking or what another knows. When playing such games, it is important to comment on your own strategy and/or on your perception of the child's strategy, as a means of making different points of view salient to the child.

Evaluating Others' Behavior. Use brief stories similar to those described in assessment, but this time you should identify *your* solution to these moral problems, again providing a reason that is *one step more advanced* than the child's own reason. A number of studies of children's moral reasoning abilities have shown that reasoning that is only slightly more advanced than a child's is the most effective impetus for developmental change. Peer interaction is thought to be particularly conducive to children's moral development for this reason. If possible, conduct discussions with a group of children regarding these moral dilemmas, and let the child learn from hearing the reasoning of his classmates.

Role-Playing. This activity works best when conducted with a group of children. Choose a short story, preferably one in which there is a conflict between two characters. This could be a scene from a book or movie or an incident from the child's own life. Have each child play a different role and, if possible, videotape their performance. Discuss each character's point of view (why each did and said what they did, what they thought caused each other's behavior, how they felt). Then switch roles. Repeat the process until each child has played and discussed each role. Begin by giving the children prepared scripts. Depending upon their age, once they have gone through one script, children may be able to write their own stories. This activity will take several sessions, especially if children begin to write their own scripts. As we note in the following session, portrayal and discussion of each character's *feelings* should be included in this exercise.

Discussions of Movies and Novels. Many movies and children's books provide excellent material for discussion of another's thoughts, intentions, feelings and behavior, and the way in which others often misinterpret a person's behavior. You may want to read aloud to the child or ask him to read a book (or see a movie or perhaps a television show) as homework. These stories—in particular, the different perspectives of the characters—should be discussed in later sessions. In this regard, books may be more effective than filmed stories, because information about the characters' thoughts and feelings often is provided directly.

CONCEPTIONS OF OTHERS' CHARACTERISTICS

Assessment

In assessing the cognitive sophistication of children's conceptions of others (and themselves) you should attend both to the *nature* of the characteristics identified (concrete to abstract) and to the *complexity* of children's characterizations (absolute to differentiated). Use Table 10.1 (Column 3) to determine the level of children's responses.

Characterizations of Others I. Ask the child for the name of her best friend (if the child says she does not have one, ask her to give a name of someone in her class whom she likes a lot). Then say, "Can you tell me what *(child's name)* is like?" and record her response. Note the extent to which the child uses *concrete attributes* (physical characteristics, possessions), *interpersonal characteristics* (friendly, nice), or statements about the other child's *beliefs, attitudes,* or *values* to describe that child. Also note the *diversity* of the child's description (for instance, how many areas of the other's personality the child mentions), and how *differentiated* are her descriptions (for example, "Sometimes she loses her temper but mostly she's pretty nice").

Next ask the child to describe an adult (teacher, parent) and note the differences between her descriptions of the child and of the adult. More sophisticated children will identify unique attributes of different people rather than using the same attributes to describe all individuals.

Characteristics of Others II. Using the list of characteristics in Table 10.2, determine how sophisticated the child can be in her conceptions of others using probe questions. For instance, if the child describes her friend as "nice" say, "You said that *(child's name)* is nice. Do you think she's mean sometimes too?" If the answer is yes, ask: "How can someone be nice and mean too?" (a more differentiated conception). Similarly, if the child uses physical characteristics to describe another, move up one level and ask "Would you say *(child's name)* is nice or not nice?" Then ask "What makes you say that *(child's name)* is nice?" or "What does *(child's name)* do that is nice?"

Intervention

Children can be helped to understand what others are like as part of some of the exercises described earlier. Activities described in the Assessment section also can be expanded.

Stories. In both the role-playing exercises described earlier and in discussions of books and movies, the child should be asked to describe what the character(s) are like—in interpersonal terms if he is sufficiently advanced. A less sophisticated child can be asked about concrete behaviors ("When the girl in the story did that, was she being friendly?") and about their generality ("Do you think she would be friendly to someone else, too?"). After some practice, the child may be able to come up with her own descriptive term for a particular behavior rather than having you supply it. The point is to help the child begin to think about others' interpersonal characteristics (or, depending on her sophistication, about others' attitudes, values, and beliefs).

Describing Others. For this activity you will need a set of file cards on which you have written or typed adjectives (for instance, those in Table 6.1) that can be used to describe a person. Include concrete and interpersonal terms (for instance, good-looking, sloppy, polite, friendly, mean), and, for older or more advanced children, terms describing attitudes or values (for instance, religious, conservative). You will also need three "key cards" on which are printed: (a) "very much like;" (b) "somewhat like"; and (c) "not at all like". In this exercise, the child will put adjective cards into the three categories labeled by the key cards to describe himself, a best or good friend, another child whom he does not like, a popular child, family members, and so forth. You should question the child about why he describes someone in a particular way ("What does [person's name] do to make you say he is polite"?), and help him to develop a more differentiated view of the person he has described ("Do you think [person's name] ever forgets to use good manners"?). This exercise will be particularly important in beginning to deal directly with the child's self-concept (by helping him develop a more differentiated view of himself) and his possibly unfavorable social comparisons (by helping him see others whom he admires in more differentiated ways).

HOMEWORK

Ask the child to notice and remember (or make notes about) a positive and negative interaction between himself and others. In addition, he may report on an interesting situation he observed between others, but one which he was not a part of himself. Have him discuss the way he and others were thinking and feeling. How could he tell? Did he make judgments on the basis of others' behavior? or their facial expressions? Did he think people accurately gauged each others' thoughts and feelings in these situations? How did their understanding or lack of understanding affect what happened? Finally, what does he think each of these individuals is like? Through your questions and comments, guide the child toward more advanced perspective-taking. Help him to see that understanding others' perspectives makes social interactions go more smoothly.

Chapter 11
Communication Skills

In order to have positive feelings about herself, a child must possess the skills necessary to get along with others. Most children seem to develop these skills naturally. However, others require more formal instruction. A child who is unsure of herself may hesitate to approach others, and therefore gains little practice in social skills. The shy child may benefit from direct instruction and practice outside of the peer group until she has gained confidence in her abilities. Children who are overbearing and aggressive also may be suffering from a lack of social skills. Instead of withdrawing, they keep interacting with other children, using whatever means (usually unpleasant) they can to stay involved in the action. Although these difficult children have not learned appropriate social skills in the peer group, they can acquire good social behavior when taken aside for step-by-step instruction. When children are able to interact successfully with others, their new capabilities may be reflected in enhanced social self-esteem.

The ability to communicate effectively with others is a large part of being able to function interpersonally. In fact, research has suggested that children who have poor communication skills tend to be less well-liked by their peers (Gottman, Gonso, & Rasmussen, 1975), and that training in conversational skills can improve social standing with peers (Ladd, 1981). Although it is not necessary for a child to be popular with everyone, an important task of childhood is learning to form positive relationships with other children. Communication skills appear to contribute to these positive social relations.

DEVELOPMENTAL CHANGES IN
COMMUNICATION ABILITIES

Those who spend time with children realize that the communication skills used naturally by children and adolescents will vary, roughly according to age. Early elementary-aged children consider others to be friends if they interact frequently with them. Their activities often involve playing side by side, sharing materials, and exchanging brief comments. This type of play soon changes to a more interactive style, with more cooperation and communication becoming necessary. Older children cite shared activities, helping, and sharing of thoughts and feelings as important dimensions of friendship, and these activities require more advanced communication abilities. Adolescents look for even more sophisticated conversational skills in their friends, as they become adept at manipulating ideas and identifying feelings in themselves and others. Due to the progressive nature of children's social communication skills, the treatment section begins with the most basic skills and builds to increased complexity.

An important element of the communication skills we describe here is children's ability to understand the perspectives of others, as outlined in chapter 10. In addition to developing social understanding, it is important that children acquire specific communication skills. The present chapter focuses specifically on listening and social behaviors that are integral to children's communication abilities.

A task for young children (approximately first and second grades) is learning to listen to others. Aside from the obvious importance of this skill for classroom learning, the ability to direct sustained attention toward peers promotes social interaction. For these young children, only brief periods of listening to peers are necessary for having fun. As children grow older and begin to have extended conversations, they develop the ability to listen for longer periods of time and they can communicate interest by head nodding, saying "uh huh," or asking questions. Asking a question is itself an important means of initiating interaction, both for very young children, who play side by side, and for older children, who may want to join an activity already in progress or initiate a conversation.

Sharing is a type of interaction valued highly by peers and adults alike. It is a very basic social skill, usually developed in the early elementary years, but—in different situations and with increased sophistication—used by people of all ages.

Another important aspect of social relationships is the exchange of compliments. Children with low self-esteem may have particular difficulties with receiving compliments, as they shrink from others' admiration when it is inconsistent with their views of themselves. Simple compliments are a feature of social interactions for children of elementary school age into adolescence.

In middle childhood, activities, games, and sports become an important arena for peer interaction. The ability to smoothly enter and leave ongoing activities is a valuable skill, which will be used into adolescence and throughout life; the activities may change but the fundamental skill remains constant.

Throughout childhood, children gradually develop the rudiments of conversation skills. Conversational exchanges are initially brief and focused on current activities. Progressively, children gain the ability to talk and think about more abstract topics—such as the future or hypothetical events and circumstances. In adolescence, youngsters may be interested in discussing the process of conversation itself. By the high school years, interactions have become longer and topics more personal and abstract.

With most communication skills, there is a progressive process of building skill components into more complex abilities. For example, listening and asking questions are important skills in their own right for young children, and later become the building blocks of conversations. If a child somehow fails to learn a basic skill, it will be difficult for him to acquire the skills that follow. It is not unusual, for example, to find that an adolescent who feels uneasy about approaching a group of peers did not master the skill of joining an activity as a child. Skill training can be very valuable in such cases, because rudimentary skills can be taught and then refined into age-appropriate social communication.

ASSESSMENT OF COMMUNICATION SKILLS

The best way to determine a child's level of communication skills is to conduct unobtrusive observations of her interactions with others. Remember, however, that she may not use a particular skill in every setting. For this reason, it may be helpful to consult teachers and parents (who may or may not be good reporters). Observing is also helpful for assessing the skill level of the peer group, so that appropriate goals can be set. When a child is not observed using a particular skill, it may be because the skill is not in her repertoire. However, another possibility is that she possesses, the skill but does not always use it. When this is the case, the role of intervention is to identify the skill, increase its salience, and provide rewards for its use.

Communication skills that children will need are identified in Table 11.1. Usually, if a child is missing a skill at an intermediate or advanced level, she will need some remedial work on the basic skills which serve as building blocks. When it is difficult to establish a child's skill level, there is no harm in beginning with the most basic skills, even if this serves only as a review.

TABLE 11.1 Communication Skills

Listening skills	
Paying attention	
Not interrupting	
Indicating understanding—	Body language and other nonverbal
Indicating interest—	expressions; asking questions
Shares	
Cooperates in group activities (including play)	
Gives compliments	
Receives compliments	
Joins group smoothly	
Ends interactions smoothly	
Developmentally appropriate content of conversations	

INTERVENTIONS

Teaching communication skills requires specific instructional methods. Initially, the helper (or a skilled child) should *model* the skill for the child. The performance should be as nearly perfect as possible, and should be followed by an explanation of how the skill steps were used to create the performance. Once the child understands the steps, she should *role play* the skill herself, using the helper or another child as the focus for the communication. The helper should give specific *feedback* about the execution of the skill, both praising the successful aspects and giving suggestions where improvement is needed. The child should try several role plays, until she is familiar and comfortable with the skill. Ideally, the role play should take place in the settings where the skill is to be used (for example, the playground or lunchroom); failing this, the setting for practice should be as similar as possible to the real-life setting. Once the child has practiced the skill through role plays, she should be encouraged to *try it in a naturalistic setting*. Discuss with her any difficulties she might face, and help her problem solve ways to deal with them. It is essential that she keep practicing the skill outside of sessions. Reward her with praise or other reinforcers for reporting that she tried out a new skill, and, when possible, reward her immediately if you observe her using the skill with other children.

A number of communication skills are described, step by step, in this section. When teaching a skill, always use modeling and role plays. It is advantageous if skilled peers can participate in role plays. To make the situation more realistic, it is sometimes helpful to provide an activity in which several children can engage while practicing the skill. In general, it is very difficult to teach communication skills effectively without the involvement of peers; try as we might, adults simply cannot adequately substitute for the genuine article. If peers are unavailable for training sessions, then practice outside sessions becomes critical, and must be strongly encouraged.

Adults can, however, be helpful in providing guidance for the use of communication skills. Even if the skill steps are perfectly mastered, there is an element of judgment involved in when, where, how, and with whom to use a skill. The appropriate use of affect, including body language and tone of voice, often speaks louder than the skill itself. Review social understanding (presented in chapter 10) with the child, and talk about the way he will be received by others if he is displaying various feelings. The emphasis should be on the most friendly way to present himself, and he may need help to develop a comfortable, genuine style of self-presentation. Discuss other fine points, such as how to decide if it is a good time to initiate communication, what are good topics for conversations or asking questions, what might be good things to share, and so forth. Think about when he can practice a new skill, and help him to choose children who will be receptive to his initial efforts. Do not forget to discuss with him things that could go wrong, and what to do if a problem occurs. In fact, the social problem solving skills presented in chapter 5 may be reviewed and incorporated here. Obviously, many subtleties exist in the use of communication skills, and it is important to help the child make these explicit. Many of the same basic skills are used by both younger and older children; it is the subleties which mark more sophisticated skill development. For the older ones, then, it is usually necessary to attend closely to the fine points of using a skill.

COMMUNICATION SKILLS

Listening

1. Look at the person who is talking.
2. Think about what the person is saying.
3. Nod head sometimes (for older children and adolescents).

Discussion points. Eye contact is especially important here. Stress the importance of not interrupting, and using appropriate facial responsiveness—smiles for happy or amusing content, for example. Try to imagine the perspective of the other person.

Asking a Question

1. Listen to what the other person is saying, or watch what the other person is doing (e.g., playing a game, working on a project).
2. Wait for a good time (i.e., when person stopped talking, or won't be disturbed if you talk).
3. Ask a question about what the person was saying or doing.

Discussion points. The content of the question will vary developmentally. For example, younger children may ask questions more concretely tied to the task at hand ("What are you drawing?") or to the content of the conversation ("What happened next?"). Adolescents may find these types of questions to be "too obvious," and may respond to more personal questions which address the person's attitudes or aptitudes ("What is it about bicycle racing that you like so much?").

Offering to Share

1. Decide if you have something somebody else might want or need (e.g., scissors or markers, or an extra cookie).
2. Decide if this is a good time to share it (Can you do without the scissors for a few minutes? Do you feel like you want to give somebody else your extra cookie today?)
3. If you want to share, offer it to somebody: "Would you like _____ (the scissors, a cookie)?"

Discussion points. It is important for the child to think about his motivation for sharing and the probable reaction of others. Some children will do anything to make friends, and their desperate attempts to "buy" others are derogated by peers. Successful sharing often comes from responding to the needs of others: noticing that another cannot continue in a project until she has access to certain materials, or receiving a direct request. Older children and adolescents may offer to share based on their understanding of another's personal qualities or interests: offering to loan a book on a topic of interest to another, allowing a friend to borrow sports equipment, clothing, or jewelry for a special occasion. For adolescents, it may be a good idea to include a reason for the offer which demonstrates the giver's understanding of the receiver ("After our conversation about sailboats, I thought you might like to read this book." "Since your sister's wedding is such a special occasion for you, I wondered if you'd like to wear that gold necklace of mine you like so much.").

Asking to Share

1. Decide if you need or want something somebody else is using.
2. Wait for a good time to ask (Has the other person had a fair chance with it?).
3. Think of a friendly way to ask ("Could I use the scissors when you're finished?" "Would you let me ride your bike?").
4. Say "thank you" when the person shares with you.

Discussion points. Again, the perspective of others is important in sharing; otherwise, a request may be perceived as selfish and inconsiderate. Younger children's sharing often takes the form of turn-taking, so fairness in length or number of turns is an issue when asking in a thoughtful manner. Adolescents may make future arrangements to share, and the needs of the other should be considered. For example, borrowing history notes over a weekend may be more considerate than asking to have them the night before a test. Also, understanding how your friend feels about lending personal items (e.g., clothing, sports equipment) can help to avoid an awkward situation where she feels imposed upon by the request. Finally, children of all ages need to understand the importance of returning a favor so that equity does not become a problem.

Giving a Compliment

1. Notice if a friend does an especially good job (or tries really hard) at something.
2. Think of a friendly thing to say to let her know you noticed ("I really like the picture you drew in art class." "Good try—you almost caught that ball." "You did a super job with that book report.").

Discussion points. A compliment should be directed toward an attribute that is valued by the recipient. Such attributes will change developmentally, initially being concrete (activities, possessions) and gradually becoming more abstract (personal qualities, abilities). Giving a compliment is similar to offering to share, in that it must be sincere and based on an understanding of the other person, and not used in order to be ingratiating.

Receiving a Compliment

1. If somebody says something nice about something you did, say "thank you".
2. Decide if you want to say something else ("I'm glad you like my drawing—I worked all weekend on it.") (for older children).

3. Do not say negative things about what you did ("It's not that great, no big deal.").

Discussion points. A child who has trouble accepting a compliment behaviorally (by saying thank you) may also find it difficult to accept praise cognitively. It may be necessary here to explore the underlying beliefs and attitudes and review the use of some cognitive strategies—i.e., self-statements, attributional style and standard setting—in order for the child to be comfortable when accepting a compliment.

Joining an Activity

1. Walk up to person or persons who are doing something you would like to join.
2. Stand on the outskirts and watch for a while.
3. Say something about what is going on ("Now it's John's turn. Good move!"). If you're not sure what to say, listen to the other kids and use them as models. Do not try to focus attention on yourself. Keep watching and commenting for a few minutes.
4. Act as much as possible like the others in the group, but do not push yourself in. Wait until they include you.

Discussion points. Joining a group is a very complicated social skill. Putallaz and Gottman (1981) have identified some of the behaviors which result in successful group entry. First, it is easier to be accepted by a group of the same social standing; a popular child will be more readily accepted by a group composed of other popular children, and the same is true for unpopular children. Children may need guidance in identifying groups which are likely to accept them. Second, it is important to determine the group's frame of reference before interacting in any way. What are the group's goals, rules, interests? Once the frame of reference is understood, the child should comment on the activity, mimicking those in the group. Any attempt to focus the group's attention on himself is likely to be ignored or rejected. Disagreements or negative comments also tend to be markedly unsuccessful. A peripheral type of engagement in the group activity should continue from the outskirts until the child is invited to join. An assertive request to be included is less likely to be successful, unless the group is composed of the child's close friends.

It is possible, of course, that the group will not include the child who is trying to become involved, and it is necessary to discuss this with him in advance. Once it seems clear that he is not going to be successful with this group (i.e., he has received outright rejections or has been ignored for five to ten minutes) he should give up gracefully. Research has not yet addressed the issue of how best to retreat from an unsuccessful attempt to join a group, but it seems clear that angry or negative responses should be avoided. A brief "see you later" should suffice for an exit line.

To date, the research on group entry has focused on younger elementary and preschool children. It may, however, be possible to extrapolate existing findings to adolescents. A relevant developmental change is that, in adolescence, group boundaries become more stable and rigid, and social status becomes highly salient. This suggests that it will be extremely difficult to join a group composed of adolescents who are more or less popular than the one trying to enter. A valuable intervention may be to talk with the adolescent about finding a compatible group of friends—people who share his values, interests, and goals. The other suggestions (determining the group's frame of reference and commenting until invited to join) may well be applicable for adolescents as well as younger children. For example, when approaching a group engaged in conversation, an adolescent could listen until he has ascertained the topic of conversation and attitudes of the speakers, then make relevant comments until the group opens to include him.

Leaving an Activity

1. Decide if it's a good time to leave (Can the activity continue without you, or will teams be uneven? Will you look like a sore loser if you leave right now?).
2. Say, "I have to go now," and give an honest reason why ("My parents want me home by 5:00." "I promised Sue I'd stop over this afternoon." "I have homework to do.").
3. As you leave, say something about seeing them another time ("See you later." "Let's play again tomorrow.").

Discussion points. The criticial factor here is to formalize the leave-taking rather than just disappearing. Any reasons given for leaving must be socially and developmentally appropriate, so as to avoid ridicule. Young children can more acceptably cite parental rules or request than can adolescents, who often feel the need to appear more autonomous. Also, a reason for leaving should not suggest that the group is boring; an adolescent who says, "I think I'll go home and clean my room" may be insulting his friends. Similarly, giving an explanation that would be perceived as unusual, negative, hostile, or weird will serve to isolate the child.

Having a Conversation

1. Decide if it's a good time (Is a person busy with somebody else? Is class about to start?). Wait until the person is available and there is enough time to talk. If you want to join a conversation a group of people have already started, use the steps for Joining an Activity.
2. Ask a question, or tell something about yourself.
3. Listen to what person says.
4. Ask another question or share something of your own, related to what person just said.
5. Continue taking turns talking.
6. If you have to end the conversation (because you have something else to do, for example), wait for person to stop talking. Then say you have to leave and give the reason why.
7. You might want to say good-bye, or say something about when you might talk again later.

Discussion points. In order to have satisfactory conversation, the child must demonstrate a genuine interest in others by asking questions and trying to understand another person. The child also needs to be involved in things that will make him of interest to others. In addition, the child will need to have developed a degree of social understanding (as discussed in chapter 10). Of special importance for conversations are recognizing the way the other person thinks and feels.

PRACTICE ACTIVITIES

For elementary age children, play activities can be arranged which will provide naturalistic opportunities for skill practice. Small groups (no larger than three or four children) are best; if skilled peers can be recruited to be part of the group, the target child will have some positive role models. Simple arts and crafts projects or games work well as activities. The skills to be practiced should be reviewed at the beginning of the activity, along with any reinforcement plan. For example, a point can be awarded each time a child uses a skill, and points can be redeemed later for small items. Begin simply, by focusing on only one or two skills, and eventually include other skills. This type of activity works well for practicing listening, asking questions, sharing, compliments, and conversations. Joining and leaving activities can be practiced by establishing a group of two or three children who are engaged in an activity while the target child waits elsewhere; then allow the target child to practice joining and leaving the group. With all types of practice activities, it is important to give immediate praise when a skill is appropriately used.

Adolescents can make good use of role playing to practice new skills. It is best to have peers, rather than adults, for practice partners if possible, but it is important not to embarrass the target youngster by choosing partners who will ridicule him. Role play situations are best chosen by the youngsters, to enhance the generalizability of practice to their real world.

In addition to role plays, practice outside of sessions is critical to acquiring these skills (see Homework).

HOMEWORK

At the end of each session, direct the child to practice new skills at home or at school. Discuss situations which may be particularly appropriate for practice. It may be useful for him to keep a log including the following information: which skill practiced; which steps used; when, where, and with whom; degree of success, how he felt about it; what he would do differently next time. As needed, the degree of detail may be increased or decreased depending upon the capabilities of the child. Review the log at the beginning of each session. You may want to provide a reinforcer of some type to increase the number of attempts.

Chapter 12
Body Image

In chapter 4, we discussed the ways in which one can identify the specific content areas in which children may experience low self-esteem. The strategy of focusing on specific self-esteem problems is exemplified by Harter's Perceived Competence Scale, which measures children's self-perceptions in social conduct, academic, appearance, and athletic domains, in addition to assessing global self-esteem (Harter, 1985). Similarly, the Five-Scale Test of Self-Esteem for Children (which can be found in Appendix) consists of measures of self-esteem in academic, social, body, and family domains, as well as an index of general self-worth. Throughout the treatment chapters we have advised that the individual child's strengths and weaknesses in these and other content areas be kept in mind and targeted with the intervention strategies provided. In this chapter, we provide an example of how the cognitive—behavioral strategies described in this manual can be applied in a specific area—that of children who have body image problems.

There is evidence that our general ideas about ourselves are based on our physical selves, including what we look like, and how we perform in the area of physical activities. For instance, a number of research studies have documented the relationship between individuals' satisfaction with their physical appearances and their self-concepts as a whole (Lerner, Karabenick, & Stuart, 1973; Rosen & Ross, 1968; Secord & Jourard, 1953). In this chapter, we first examine the nature of children's body images at different developmental periods and how it relates to their general self-esteem. We then review both means of assessing how children view their physical selves and intervention strategies for dealing with problems in this area.

DEVELOPMENTAL CHANGES IN
BODY IMAGE

Youngsters' ideas about their physical selves show how tremendous changes from infancy and early childhood through adolescence, and the relationship between body concept and self-esteem also seems to change developmentally. The task for infants is to learn to recognize themselves, to distinguish their own motor activities and their consequences from those of the world around them, and to gain control over their bodies so that they can direct their own activities. By early childhood, children generally have accomplished the former two of these abilities, and they continue during the school-age years to develop and refine physical and gross motor abilities. As such, young children's views of their physical selves tend to center around their physical activities and abilities (Keller, Ford, & Meacham, 1978). As youngsters approach adolescence, however, their body images become increasingly tied to their appearance and their beliefs about their physical attractiveness.

In our earlier discussion of developmental changes in adolescence (see chapter 3), we described young teens' preoccupation with self and their exaggerated ideas about their place in other persons' thoughts. The physical changes that become apparent as teenagers go through puberty are the focus of intense interest and concern to the teens themselves. In their egocentrism, teenagers may believe that these physical character-istics and changes are equally salient and interesting to others around them.

The developmental changes of puberty, however, appear to be differ-entially important for females and males. That is, in adolescence females' evaluations of their physical attractiveness are the most important predic-tors of their self-concept scores, whereas it is males' ratings of their self-effectiveness that better predict boys' self-concept scores (Lerner, Orlos, & Knapp, 1976).

In fact, several lines of research suggest that physical development and body concept in adolescence have very different meanings for girls and boys. In adolescence, for instance, girls are more critical of their bodies than are boys. In fact, some researchers have suggested that the high incidence of eating disorders such as bulimia and anorexia among ado-lescent females in our contemporary culture arise when, during puberty, girls express negative feelings about body fat and the changing bodily proportions associated with normal sexual development (Dornbusch, Carlsmith, Duncan, Gross, Marto, Ritter, & Siegel-Gorelick, 1984); girls with eating disorders often display low self-esteem ("Eating Disorders 'Normal,' " 1985).

The rate of physical maturation during puberty also has important psychosocial consequences which differ for girls and boys. Early maturation in girls, for instance, seems to be associated with emotional and behavioral problems, including truancy and substance abuse (Magnusson, Stattin, & Allen, 1985). These girls also tend to be less popular with their peers. Moreover, the self-esteem of attractive girls tends to be affected more negatively by pubertal changes than is that of less attractive girls (Zakin, Blyth, & Simmons, 1984). Researchers have suggested that this is because the self-concepts of attractive girls are more closely linked to their physical appearances. For girls, in general, the message society clearly conveys is that "what is beautiful is good" (Dion, Berscheid, & Walster, 1972, p. 285). And indeed, studies of adolescent peer groups show that for girls, popularity is strongly connected to physical attractiveness.

The case for boys is somewhat different. In contrast to girls, boys who go through puberty early relative to their male peers seem to have an edge over other boys (Jones & Bayley, 1950; Mussen & Jones, 1957). Given that girls tend to mature earlier than boys, boys who reach puberty at a younger age may in fact be "on time" relative to their female peers. Moreover, because males are "supposed to be" larger and stronger than females, a late-maturing boy may be at an extreme disadvantage when it comes to developing heterosexual relationships in adolescence. Finally, for boys, popularity with peers is associated with athletic ability and, to a lesser extent, appearance. The physical growth and secondary sexual characteristics that develop during puberty consequently may become significant factors in how and whether a teenager establishes himself in the peer group. Longitudinal studies underscore the importance of the adolescent male's experiences. Some work shows, for instance, that males who mature at a later age suffer in terms of their self-concepts and social relations, and that these problems persist into adulthood (Ames, 1957; Jones, 1965; Weatherly, 1964).

In sum, youngsters' body images appear to be central to how they see themselves, to how others treat them, and, in turn, to how they relate to others. As such, they may need to be taught how to make the most of their physical assets through lessons in grooming, hygiene, exercise, and skills training.

Perhaps more important, however, is what preadolescents and adolescents *think* about their bodies. Some research evidence as well as clinical anecdotes suggest that some youngsters form distorted impressions of themselves, and may see themselves much more negatively than others see them. As was mentioned, a most extreme example of this potential problem is seen in the high rate of eating disorders exhibited by adolescent girls in our society. These girls not only may hold distorted

ideas about how fat and unattractive they are; they also may hold impossibly high standards for how they believe they ought to look. Along these
same lines, youngsters may hold very high standards for what they
should be able to do with their bodies, comparing their abilities against
those of top athletes in the nation rather than others their own age. Thus,
one focus of intervention from a *cognitive–behavioral perspective* is to help
youngsters to examine, and possibly modify, standards for their physical
selves. In the following pages we describe a set of strategies geared in
this direction.

PHYSICAL ATTRACTIVENESS

As in other areas of self-esteem, two factors we must consider in assessing body image problems regarding physical attractiveness are: (1) the
child's actual appearance; and (2) the child's standards for how he or she
would like to look.

One possible basis of body image problems is that children may be
ignorant about what standards their peer group holds for physical attractiveness, in terms of such features as hair style, dress, and hygiene, for
example. Alternatively, although they may be aware of the "look" that
is in vogue, youngsters may be unaware of what they can do through
diet, exercise, cosmetics, and so forth to best achieve their desired
appearance. Thus, one set of strategies for intervention is directed toward
educating youngsters about others' standards for physical appearance
and about the means through which they might enhance their own physical attractiveness.

Another set of strategies focuses on youngsters whose standards for
their physical appearance may be too high. As discussed in chapter 3,
self-esteem can be thought of as the discrepancy between the "real"
and the "ideal" self. When it comes to physical attractiveness, societal
standards of beauty as portrayed on television and in magazine ads may
be the basis of one's "ideal" appearance. Yet these standards may be
difficult to achieve. Thus, another strategy for promoting positive self-
esteem is to alter an individual's standards for what she or he should
look like.

A related problem of some youngsters is that they actually may distort
their images of themselves and see themselves as less attractive then they
really are. This can happen as a result of setting extremely high standards
for themselves, as we have mentioned. Alternatively, youngsters may be
"centered" on some small or imagined "defect" (for instance, big ears, a
gap between the front teeth, or too many freckles), which is virtually
unnoticeable to others but which colors the child's entire perception of

himself. This tendency to focus or "center" on a single factor while ignoring the larger picture is a characteristic of young children's thinking style. A related form of egocentric thought emerges again in full force in early adolescence (see chapter 3) when adolescents seem to believe that they are the focus of everyone's attention (i.e., the "imaginary audience"). In such cases, refocusing strategies are an important intervention approach that can be used to change the object(s) of an individual's attention to enhance her or his sense of self-worth. For instance, a youngster might be encouraged to focus on a good figure or an attractive smile rather than a nose of the wrong shape or size that is making her feel badly about herself.

Refocusing also is a very useful strategy for youngsters who actually may not fit peer or societal norms for what constitutes "good looks." For these youngsters, as we noted earlier, exercise, diet, or grooming programs sometimes may be helpful. Beyond these actual changes in behavior, however, cognitive restructuring exercises may help to lower youngsters' standards for their physical appearance and, perhaps more importantly, refocus their attention from their appearance to some other domain in which they may be particularly competent (e.g., academically, interpersonally, athletically). In this way, some other domain may become central to youngsters' general sense of themselves.

Before outlining intervention exercises, one caveat is in order. The widespread prevalence of eating disorders such as bulimia and anorexia has become the focus of public attention and researchers have suggested that these young people (most likely girls) tend to hold distorted images of their bodies. These youngsters seem to believe that they are unattractive and overweight when, in fact, they may be quite attractive, and, in the case of individuals with anorexia, grossly underweight. Although self-esteem issues may be central to these problems, eating disorders (similarly to anxiety disorders) constitute a specialized and usually extreme form of adjustment difficulties that we cannot adequately cover in this manual. Although some of the cognitive behavioral strategies we discuss here may be useful for treating eating disorders, more specialized programs are available and for such problems we strongly recommend consultation with a professional who has experience with these problems.

ASSESSMENT OF BODY IMAGE

Prior to planning intervention strategies, it is important to determine just how youngsters feel about their physical appearance and why they feel the way they do. You may want to use a scale such as the one developed by Harter (1985) to begin to get a picture of children's feelings about their physical appearance. As we mentioned earlier, this question-naire focuses on children's perceived competence in the areas of athletics, academics, conduct, peer relations, and general self-worth, in addition to their perceptions of their physical attractiveness. Thus, it may be a useful starting place for assessing self-esteem problems in a number of domains. Scale items in the appearance area focus on issues such as facial features and body build, and will provide a good beginning point for discussing in greater detail the child's evaluations of his or her appearance.

Alternatively, you can talk to children about their body image by asking questions such as "What do you like best/least about your looks?" "What do you like best/least about your body?" Clearly this will not be an easy issue for most children to discuss. Many children, especially as they approach adolescence, may feel extraordinarily sensitive about what adults would see as fairly insignificant physical features. For example, a good-looking, well-built fifth grade boy interviewed by one of the authors was preoccupied by a tiny gap between his two front teeth that colored his entire perception of his physical attractiveness. This "defect" made him feel quite unattractive and he was so embarrassed about it that it took a good deal of time before he would actually admit the source of his body image problem. Once this was out in the open, it was relatively easy to deal with this self-esteem problem through the standard setting and refocusing exercises outlined below.

In addition to gauging children's subjective evaluations of their appearance, you also will need to develop a more objective rating of their physical attractiveness including facial features, body build, and grooming. This too can be a difficult task, largely because adults may have a very different idea about how attractive a child is than do the child's peers. Thus, a more objective picture of the child's attractiveness should be developed keeping in mind peer norms regarding hair style, cosmetic use, dress, grooming, and rate of physical growth and develop-ment. When working with adolescents, you should keep in mind the discussion of maturation rate in adolescence at the beginning of this chapter.

INTERVENTIONS TO ENHANCE BODY IMAGE

Once you understand children's evaluations of their attractiveness and you have a more general sense of how they probably are perceived by others (their peers in particular), you are in a better position to plan your approach to intervention. Decisions about intervention will be based on:

(a) whether children can benefit from changing their overt behaviors relative to their appearance, such as dress, personal hygiene, diet, or exercise; or (b) whether children's internalized standards for how they ought to look—that is, their ideals for themselves—should be modified. For many children, a balance between these two approaches will be most appropriate.

Given the orientation of this manual, it would be inappropriate to delve into issues of grooming, hygiene, exercise, and diet or other means of helping children actually alter their physical appearance. Cognitive – behavioral strategies, such as self-guiding speech and self-reinforcement can be very important for establishing new behavioral regimens such as dieting or carrying out an exercise program. Such programs, however, are beyond the scope of this book.

Instead our focus here is on changing how children think about their physical appearance. Your assessment should have provided you with information about the extent to which: (a) children are ignorant about norms for personal appearance; and (b) children hold impossibly high standards for their own appearance. As we noted before, in most cases this will not be a choice of one option or the other, but some combination of both types of problems.

Teaching Norms About Personal Appearance

For the child who seems unaware about norms for dress or hygiene, a straightforward discussion is in order. You can talk to the child about what most youngsters his or her age do with regard to their physical appearance, and the ways in which the child herself differs from that standard. It also is important to present information to the child about the potential consequences of his or her current behaviors regarding physical appearance, including the ways in which the child is perceived by others (for instance, in the case of a child with poor hygiene) or the effects on the child's physical health (for instance, in the case of a child who is overweight). In our opinion, however, with the exception of extreme cases, such information should *not* be given to children in the form of arguments for promoting behavior changes. Although it is realistic to acknowledge the impact one's physical appearance has on how one is perceived and often treated by others, we believe it is *inappropriate* to attempt to impose on children conformity to fairly arbitrary standards of beauty.

A case in point was an intellectually gifted school-age girl with whom one of us worked. This child was ridiculed by her peers for the kinds of clothes she wore (clean, well-fitting, comfortable, but not what her peers were wearing) and her hair style (no braids, barrettes, mousse, or perm, as were popular with the other girls in her class). In one session we discussed in detail the strategies this child could use to alter her appearance in ways that would conform to the other girls' standards. A week later this child confided that she had thought about our conversation and tried out some of the strategies we had discussed. She had decided, however, that the effort it took to become one of the crowd kept her from doing other things that she really enjoyed and, ultimately, she opted to return to her unfashionable appearance. Unfortunately, not all children can face the possibility of peer rejection with such equanimity. Again, the important point is that norms about appearance often are somewhat arbitrary and the interventionist must take care that she is not preaching conformity for its own sake. In short, an important goal is to help a child see how she is perceived by others (see chapter 10 on social understanding) and the potential consequences of her behavior (see chapter 5 for a discussion of social problem solving). In addition, you should be ready to support that child in making decisions about her personal standards for her appearance, as we discuss in the following pages.

Modifying Standards for Physical Attractiveness

Not only are standards for physical attractiveness often arbitrary, but a desirable "look" also may be extremely difficult to achieve. For example, youngsters may suffer from low self-esteem because they can be satisfied only if they are the best looking boy or girl in their class or if they have the body build or hair style of a favorite television actor or top model. In other words, they set unrealistic standards for themselves and believe that they either are or are not attractive depending on whether they meet those standards. This absolutist, "all or nothing" kind of thinking is very characteristic of school-age children in particular, and, as noted in chapter 9, has been labeled "dichotomous thinking". In chapter 9, we also discussed the issue of standard setting in general, and in the following pages we will consider ways to apply relevant interventions in the area of body image problems.

Identification and modification of standards. As we discussed in chapter 9, standard setting involves two kinds of cognitions which may be targets of intervention: (a) the implicit or explicit standards children hold about themselves; and (b) the self-evaulations that arise from comparing actual performance against the standard.

In intervention you should follow the steps outlined on pages 83 through 86, which help children become aware of the standards they hold and the effects of their failure to meet those standards. It will be important to ask children to evaluate multiple aspects of their body image (hair, facial features, height, weight, dress, hygiene). This way they begin to appreciate that although they may fail to meet their own expectations in regard to some aspects of physical appearance, they may feel quite positively about other aspects. It will be very important to help children identify the self-statements and attributions associated with their "successes" and "failures" as these will be important targets for intervention.

Modifying attributions. Another goal is to modify those attributions that arise when youngsters fail to achieve their standards for attractiveness. Your goal is to help them realize that their "failure" is not caused by some deeply rooted, personal defect.

For the child who is overweight or the one called "toothpick" by her peers, for the child with an active case of acne or buck teeth, it is important to move them away from *stable (permanent)* and *global* attributions about their appearance ("I'm ugly and I'll always be ugly"; "I'm ugly and therefore worthless") to specific and time-limited concepts ("I'm overweight now but I'll look better after I diet"). When possible, the attribution retraining can fit within the method described in chapter 7.

Homework for Practicing Attributions. Children will need to monitor their feelings and thoughts about their body image as part of their homework assignment. They should keep track of when disturbing feelings about their body image actually arise, and what kinds of attributions they make at those times. You will need to model and role play ways that youngsters can work on altering those attributions, using the self-reinforcement procedure we have described in other chapters.

Refocusing. Some children may develop global attributions about themselves on the basis of their physical appearance (for example, children who feel they are almost worthless because they are unattractive). For these youngsters, strategies which change the focus of children's standards may be useful. Refocusing strategies may be aimed at: (1) changing which *physical* attributes form the basis of a child's self-evaluation ("I may not have a very pretty face, but I have a good figure"); (2) altering the domains a child focuses on in developing his general sense of self-worth ("I may not be very attractive, but I do really well at my school work"); or (3) changing the reference group that provides the basis of a child's standards ("I may not be as attractive as the prettiest girls in the class, but compared to most kids my age I look okay").

Because children and young teens still may be very "concrete" in their thinking, it may be difficult for them to think of standards as somewhat arbitrary social conventions. Thus, a first step in helping youngsters "refocus" may be to educate them, for instance, about the cultural and historical relativity of societal standards of beauty. Concrete thinking also may mean that children somehow believe that external appearances *necessarily* tell us something about a person's general character. Obviously, many adults suffer from a similar perspective on the world, but it may be more powerful in youngsters at this stage of cognitive development. Discussing the fallacy of this belief will be an important strategy in altering the standards of some children. You also can provide concrete examples of individuals who do not conform to children's expectations about the equivalent of goodness and beauty. Finally, a child may profit from discussion with peers whose ideas about these issues are slightly more advanced than the child's own thinking style.

Modifying self-statements. Another procedure, similar to what Canfield and Wells (1976) have called "mirror–mirror," can be used with school age children to help them change the way they talk and think about themselves. In this procedure, a child stands in front of a full-length mirror and tells you what he or she sees.

To begin this exercise, first tell the youngster to stand in front of the mirror and to close her eyes. When she opens them, she should look into the mirror and very quickly tell you what she sees first. The next step is to instruct the child to tell you what she likes best about what she sees in the mirror. The process may be facilitated by asking questions such as, "If the mirror could talk to you, what do you think it would say?" or "What doesn't the mirror know about you?" Because the major purpose of this procedure is to encourage the child to enhance her self-esteem, it is very important to facilitate the expression of positive things that the child sees in the mirror. Obviously this will be difficult with a child suffering from low self-esteem, and it usually will take a great deal of encouragement and prompting. You should be prepared to describe several positive features that you see in the child. Even though this may be a somewhat embarrassing, difficult, or tedious process for the child, we have found it to be an effective way to get the child to focus upon the physical attractiveness that, in fact, is really there.

Canfield and Wells (1976) suggested that the effectiveness of the "mirror–mirror" exercise can be enhanced by the use of what they call a "strength bombardment" procedure. They suggest that the child ask four or five good friends to stand behind him as he sits or stands in front of the mirror. The youngsters should stand in a pattern that allows the "target" child to see all of their faces in the mirror. The "target" child then looks at himself in the mirror and tells himself positive things regarding himself: nothing else, just the positive things. The youngsters who are standing around him and looking into the mirror are there to provide him with additional positive things that he can say about himself. They do this when the child himself runs out of positive things to say. They need not rush in, but when there is a pause, they should be prepared to offer positive suggestions. After the first child is done, other children should take turns being the "target." This will keep the child who is the focus of intervention from being overly uncomfortable or embarrassed by the exercise.

Although this exercise may be a little difficult at first, many children seem to enjoy the experience. Canfield and Wells suggest allowing about five minutes for this exercise, although our experience in working with children individually indicates that it may take a little longer because it is difficult for the children to get started. Once they do get started, however, they enjoy it so much that it will probably take a few more minutes in order for them to run out of positive things to say. Although there is no empirical evidence to support the effectiveness of this procedure, indirect support for it can be derived from the effectiveness of group work with children which focuses on the enhancing effects of other children giving an individual positive feedback about various attributes. It seems this would be a particularly effective strategy when youngsters are physically attractive and are distorting their image of themselves; the input from the other children can very easily focus on the positive attributes and perhaps serve the purpose of stopping the child's distorting.

PHYSICAL PERFORMANCE

A second area that plays a major role in the relationship between body image and self-esteem is the area of performance in physical activities. These activities may include sports, artistic endeavors such as dance, and other kinds of athletic activities. As we noted earlier, there seem to be gender differences in the importance of physical performance for self-esteem. That is, this area seems to be somewhat more important to boys (especially in regard to peer popularity) and the importance of this area seems to increase as children approach adolescence.

As is the case with physical attractiveness, there are a number of strategies that may be employed to enhance youngsters' perceptions of themselves in the area of physical performance and body image. These include direct training in skills necessary for competence in this area (e.g., lessons, practice for a given sport) and the possibility of modifying a youngster's standards for success. In addition, an important strategy is to teach young people the importance of matching their physical assets and skills with their interest areas (a form of "refocusing"). Thus, a boy who has a small body build may have a very difficult time competing in football or basketball but may do very well in other sports, such as tennis or gymnastics. In fact, his particular stature may be an asset for some sports. If this boy believes that he can only be worthwhile and acceptable if he excels in one particular sport, however, then physical performance is likely to be an area of self-esteem problems. Recall that "refocusing" strategies involve reorienting youngsters' attention away from a particular domain in which they may not be "naturally" competent or effective toward one in which success comes more readily.

As was the case with physical attractiveness, there are a number of areas in which education and changes in overt behavior may play a significant role in enhancing self-esteem regarding physical performance. Obviously, it is extremely important for youngsters to physically prepare themselves for the tasks they plan to undertake. You can talk to children about the importance of factors such as nutrition and eating habits, sleeping patterns, general physical conditioning through exercise, and practice and coaching for specific skills. Although cognitive behavioral strategies may help a child maintain a healthy behavioral regimen (e.g., by using self-statements in self-control and self-reinforcement to maintain a diet or exercise program), such broad-scale programs are beyond the scope of this manual. It will be important, however, to evaluate whether the child understands the significance of the physical factors that are prerequisite to success in the area of physical performance.

As with physical attractiveness, the internal standards youngsters set for themselves are a primary target for intervention. You can assess children's perceptions of their abilities using the athletic competence subscale of Harter's (1985) Perceived Competence Scale, and also question youngsters in a more general way about their strengths and weaknesses in this area. In addition, you will need to develop a more objective rating of their capabilities (such as by observing a child with her peers on the playing field, talking to a coach or physical education teacher, and so forth). With both sets of information, you will be in a position to determine: (a) whether children are realistically evaluating their performance, which falls short of common standards; or (b) whether they are "distorting" their performance ability, such as by believing they are less competent than they really are, possibly because their standards are too high.

For the former group, when children actually do seem to fall short of realistic expectations for youngsters their age, exercises that help them modify their standards or refocus their self-evaluations will be useful. These exercises would include: (a) *lowering standards* to what may be realistically expected, given a child's "natural" abilities (e.g., the child with a small body build who wants to play basketball or football); (b) *changing standards*, so that a child sets a realistic, individualized goal rather than comparing his performance against that of the top athlete in his class, in his school, or on television; (b) *refocusing*, so that a child's self-evaluations come primarily from how she performs skills that she can carry out successfully and competently (for instance, her self-perceptions are derived from how well she does at soccer, *not* tennis; self-evaluations come from how well a boy performs academically, not athletically); and (d) *modifying attributions*, so that when children are unsuccessful they do *not* infer that their failure results from a negative attribute that is permanent, global, and unchangeable. Your goal here is to help children acknowledge both their abilities and limitations in a realistic way without being devastated by failures.

For children who seem to be distorting their actual level of ability, exercises that require children to openly express what they are good at or which allow them to hear their good qualities expressed by others (as in "mirror–mirror") may be effective intervention strategies. Again, the goal is to change children's "self-statements," or the ways in which they talk and think about themselves.

Chapter 13

Special Issues

Even a structured treatment package does not provide for every contingency; there are always questions, problems, and issues which arise and must be addressed outside of the session-by-session program. In this chapter we will address some of the issues and problems which may occur while using this structured intervention for children with low self-esteem.

TERMINATION (SAYING GOOD-BYE)

After working with a youngster for a period of weeks or months, you will necessarily have formed a special bond with her. She has probably given you access to many of her most private thoughts and feelings, and has developed with you what may be an unusually trusting relationship. Aside from your professional role in the treatment, you have probably developed some feelings of attachment to her as well. Because of these special ties you have created, it is important to handle leave-taking with care.

Paradoxically, the end of the intervention program is best addressed before beginning and throughout the process of treatment. It may be possible at the outset to determine the amount of time you will be working together; a structured program such as this facilitates an estimation of treatment length. When first explaining the purpose of working together, you can give her an idea about the time frame. Thereafter, you can periodically comment on how much time remains in your "contract." As the time for termination draws near, perhaps six weeks ahead, begin mentioning on a weekly basis the fact that you will be ending soon. Adolescents can be given a termination date, but younger children should be told, "We will meet (__) more times after today." Do take time to answer questions and to allow the youngster to express her feelings about leaving you. It is very common for both anger and sadness to be part of a response to ending the relationship; if you do not hear about such feelings, you may want to say, "I wonder if you're feeling sad about having to stop seeing me," or "Often, kids get mad about having to stop these meetings." Don't be put off if anger is directed at you. It is important for the child to see you accept her feelings about the process of treatment, just as you have been accepting of her thoughts and feelings about other areas of her life.

The final session should be reserved just for wrapping up and saying good-bye. You may want to ask if there have been other times when she has had to say good-bye to someone she never saw again, and how that felt. You should ask her what memories of your time together she will take away with her; this will be an important way of solidifying what she has learned from you. Do not hesitate to tell her some of your own feelings about leaving and the work you have done together. Younger children may enjoy exchanging a token such as good-bye cards, which you would make for each other in the session. However you structure this last meeting, the focus must be on the feelings you have about having worked together and about leaving each other.

The lesson to be learned through a properly handled termination is that the child has gotten more from you than the set of skills which have been the primary focus of your efforts. Throughout the intervention, you have provided a model for consistency and trust in a relationship, and you have given the child an opportunity to practice being in this kind of relationship. The fact that you have valued the child, strengths and weaknesses alike, may very well have enhanced her self-esteem.

TROUBLESHOOTING

Back-Up Reinforcement: Enlisting Participation

Although most children are willing to participate in a program such as this, it is essential on occasion to establish a back-up reinforcement system to develop and maintain attendance in the program. This system should be employed only when encouragement and social support for the program are not strong enough to promote participation.

A typical back-up reinforcement system requires the identification of reinforcers for a particular child, the development of the contingency system, and the clear explanation of the system to the child. Reinforcers vary according to age level and the specific child. The range of reinforcers includes more time with peers, more "free" time, "stars" for attendance, and even primary reinforcers such as food.

The reinforcement system must be developed *a priori* and clearly explained to the child. The target behaviors must be defined, and the contingency between the behavior and the reinforcer must be developed and explained to the child.

It is also important to try to fade the system as soon as possible. In most cases, the child will come to enjoy the activities of the program; even with resistant children, it nearly always becomes inherently or intrinsically reinforcing, and the external reinforcement system can be gradually dropped.

Working in Harmony with Existing Systems

It is important to remember that change by the child always occurs in a context. This means that if the program is effective the child should present differently in the classroom, on the playground, and at home. In order to facilitate treatment effectiveness and maintain the obtained treatment results, it is important to have the full cooperation of all school personnel and family members.

When a program occurs at school, it is typical for the administration to approve the program. It is not unusual, however, for the administration to be unaware of the details of various counseling activities. In a program like this one, in which the student leaves the classroom for a substantial period of time, it is important for the teacher and appropriate administrators to know the objectives and details of the intervention program. The administration needs to understand the philosophy of the program, be able to represent it to parents, and back it up with appropriate support, including time, space, and public statements. It is essential to work closely with the teacher(s) so the new skills learned via the program can be reinforced in the classroom and playground setting. The extent of the child's change can be substantially enhanced by the strong support of a concerned and caring teacher; likewise, a program's effectiveness can be completely undermined by a poorly informed and/or uncooperative teacher.

It is also important for the parents to be informed fully about the child's participation. From an ethical/legal viewpoint, the parents must know in what areas the program is helping their child change. Furthermore, many of the self-defeating cognitive and behavioral patterns of low self-esteem children may have developed from self-defeating models in the home. Even though change in the parents can be difficult to achieve, their increased awareness and understanding of the child's difficulties can lead to support for this opportunity for the child to change and grow. This makes it easier for the child to change and improves the likelihood of the child's cooperation in the program.

When a program begins, it is essential to enlist not only the cooperation of the student but also the cooperation of the family, teacher(s), and administration. This should provide for better cooperation and needed support throughout the program.

When This Program is Not Enough

It is possible that a child with serious deficits in one (or more) of the skills taught here may need additional work beyond what is provided within this program. Appendix 13.1 contains a bibliography of treatment programs which target in a comprehensive manner many of the skills addressed in this program. You may consult these materials if additional assistance is needed with a particular type of intervention.

VARIATIONS IN USE OF THE PROGRAM

Groups

Although this program was designed with an individual approach in mind, many of the targeted skills lend themselves quite readily to instruction and practice in small groups. The topics of social understanding and communication skills are actually enhanced by using peers as learning partners. Youngsters of all ages can benefit from a group model.

Groups should be kept small, with three to four members. The small size becomes more important as the degree of self-esteem difficulty of the members increases. The group should be ongoing and consistent, without changes in membership, so that a sense of comfort and trust can develop among the children.

Selecting the right combination of children is crucial to the success of a group approach. It is best if there are no large disparities in skill level, because it will make instruction more difficult (i.e., the different needs of the children will be hard to address), will reduce the children's ability to learn from one another, and may create discomfort for them. If possible, group members should be at about the same level, developmentally and skill-wise. Small differences in ability can provide opportunities to learn through modeling; ideally, each child would have a peer model who is "one step up" on the ladder of skill development. Of course, even within the same child there may be differential development of skills. For example, one child may excel at cognitive strategies to enhance self-esteem but falter with behavioral social skills, while another child of the same age may show the reverse pattern of abilities.

Few changes need to be made in the basic skill program when working with a group. The introduction of a new skill can be done in a didactic manner, and then the individuals can take turns with the intervention exercises. Often, a peer pair can work (with guidance) as the helper-child pair would have operated. This is particularly valuable when role-playing to practice social skills. Alternatively, a group discussion, with each child contributing his own individual perspective, can be a powerful means of learning in a supportive environment. Chapter 11, Communication Skills, suggests other ways to use group instruction in that area. With a little creativity, the treatment program can be easily adapted to group instruction.

An additional element to attend to is the group process—the developing relationships among group members. Initially, you may have to schedule some noninstructional time for the children to get to know one another; it could be very difficult for them to plunge into the lessons, which require a large degree of self-disclosure, in the presence of unfamiliar people. It is a good idea to set the stage for group behavior by establishing rules or policies. Allow the group to determine the rules, but be sure they include: (a) respecting what others say without ridicule, and (b) confidentiality—nothing discussed in the group can be told outside. Young children may need some rules governing behavior, such as "no name-calling" and "no hitting." As time passes, relationships will deepen, engendering closeness as well as conflicts. Take time to address conflicts when they occur, and try to help the individuals reach a resolution. One of the major rewards of group treatment is the important lessons group members learn about being in relationships with others, and it is important to remember that this aspect is always functioning, even while the group's attention is focused on skill training.

There are many benefits in using a group model while teaching skills to enhance self-esteem. Group members learn to relate to peers, and they discover that they are not alone or unusual in having a negative self-image. Opportunities for modeling abound, and socially oriented areas are, in fact, best taught with peer partners. Further, professional time is efficiently utilized, a not inconsequential issue given the often inadequate resources available to children. Groups, however, are not ideal for every situation. Some children are too unruly, and others too withdrawn, for group-based instruction. In addition, if the proper group composition cannot be created with the available children, an individual approach would be advisable. As long as the clinician is able to be flexible, the program can be applied to both group and individual modalities with positive results.

Classroom

It is possible to adapt this intervention program for use as an in-class curriculum. There will necessarily be less focus on each individual, which will probably result in less powerful learning effects than would be obtained with an individual or small-group approach. However, for children who have only mild problems with self-esteem, classroom use of the program could be a successful way to help alleviate those self-esteem difficulties, and perhaps could also be employed in a preventive manner.

Initially, it will be important to set the stage for the introduction to the program. Specific time periods once or twice a week should be scheduled so that the children will know to anticipate the lessons. A comfortable environment must be created—sitting on the floor in a circle, for example. Give a rationale description of the program: "It is important for each of us to like ourselves, but sometimes that is hard to do. Today we will begin learning some new ways to feel comfortable with ourselves." As was discussed for small groups, work together to establish rules for the group. In a classroom of young children, a procedure for taking turns when speaking may have to be established; for example, possession of a specified object entitles the child to speak, and all others must listen and wait their turn. During the first session, it may be a good idea to "warm up" by staging a group discussion. A topic as simple as "something good and something bad about today" can give each child a chance to speak and be heard while the group practices using the rules and becomes accustomed to this unfamiliar activity. Remember from the outset to reinforce appropriate behavior by attending to it—a comment, a smile, a touch—and ignore inappropriate behavior. This will help your group to learn "good manners" and good working skills quickly.

When using the program sessions, you can use a combination of instructional methods. Didactic presentations or group discussions will work well with many topics. Role-playing can be set up for two children at a time (perhaps adding a third as the skill is mastered) to perform in the center of the circle, with the rest of the group watching for elements of good skill use. Adolescents may enjoy keeping a log of their reactions to the program and their attempts to practice new skills. Above all, efforts should be made to keep the sessions varied and interesting.

Some special opportunities are available when an entire class is involved in a self-esteem enhancement program. If the teacher is the person leading the group, she can make enormous strides in encouraging the use of new skills by prompting and reinforcing skill use every day. If she notices a child using a skill, she can praise him for it. Alternatively, when an ideal opportunity arises for using a particular skill she can prompt a child to use it, and then praise the child's effort. A second advantage of classroom-based instruction is the opportunity to teach powerful lessons in social understanding. When ripe moments present themselves, the teacher can ask children to identify their own cognitive or emotional perspective on the situation, thus promoting sensitivity toward one another. Ultimately this can lead to a caring, respectful classroom atmosphere, which may, in itself, provide a valuable source of self-esteem enhancement.

FOLLOW-UP AND MAINTENANCE

A primary concern should always be the maintenance of gains made in treatment, yet this is one of the more difficult aspects of any intervention. This section will discuss several methods of encouraging a child's continued use of the skills he has learned from the structured treatment program.

Booster Sessions

Periodically, you could meet with the child to reassess his ability to use his new skills in a way which enhances his self-esteem. Such an assessment could be informal, where you talk with him about how things are going in his life, or may have more formal components, such as the self-esteem tests mentioned in chapter 4 and/or the assessment strategies outlined in the intervention chapters. You might want to schedule this type of evaluation in advance, say, at two, six, and twelve months following termination. It may be wise to plan a follow-up contact at times which would be predictably stressful. For example, the transition between elementary and junior high grades is notoriously hard on self-esteem (Rosenberg, 1979). Another strategy would be to allow the child to initiate the contact when he feels the need to "brush up" on his skills.

Once the areas of strength and weakness have been identified, you may need to spend one, two, or three sessions to regain an acceptable skill level. In addition to targeting problem areas, be sure to support and reinforce the child's successful use of other skills. In any booster session, an emphasis should be placed on helping the child to adapt previously acquired skills to the demands of his changing environment and development. Once he has managed to accomplish such a transition, his capability for smoothly negotiating future life changes should be improved.

Teacher and Parent Involvement

Teachers and parents, as significant adults in the child's life, can have a positive influence on his ability to continue using appropriate skills. In order to do so, they must have a thorough understanding of the skills which have been taught and of the individual child's level of performance. Motivated parents or teachers may want to read this book, especially the intervention chapters, or you may want to present the material yourself. Other resources may be useful as well; one in particular is the Clabby and Elias (1985) book, *Teach Your Child Decision Making*, which is designed to help parents learn to promote social problem solving in their children.

Teachers and parents also need to learn appropriate methods of encouraging good skill use, as discussed in chapter 2 and throughout the intervention chapters. *Accentuate the positive* is the first and most important rule. If they see him using a skill well, they should use *positive reinforcement* by commenting, praising, or otherwise recognizing in a positive manner that he has done a good job. When he is partially successful, they should praise the positive aspects of his performance. Later on, they can use problem solving strategies together to decide how he can improve his use of that skill, or how he could have used it more successfully. In appropriate situations, adults can *prompt* the use of a skill and then *reinforce* him for it. *Modeling* these skills themselves is yet another way for adults to promote the child's acquisition and use of new behavior. As teacher and parents continue to use these strategies, they enhance the child's likelihood of maintaining new abilities over time and generalizing their use to different settings.

Classroom Awareness

A teacher can encourage positive self-esteem in her classroom just by making it a topic for discussion and a focus of activities. Because a teacher's comments can carry a lot of weight with children, she can be very influential by suggesting self-esteem-enhancing interpretations of events, using the cognitive strategies in the treatment program. She can also foster among the students an attitude of sensitivity to others, thereby creating a classroom atmosphere which encourages respect for self and others. Finally, there are endless possibilities for classroom activities which have a goal of promoting healthy self-images in students. A good resource is Canfield's (1976) book, *100 Ways to Enhance Self-Concept in the Classroom*. Such strategies for classroom awareness of children's need for positive self-esteem could benefit a recent "graduate" of the structured treatment program as well as the rest of the class.

Afterword

The treatment program presented in this book deals with many aspects of self-esteem, and therefore may appear to be a conglomeration of treatment perspectives which have little relation to one another. The purpose of this Afterword is to demonstrate the ways in which these multiple areas can be integrated into a coherent program. Earlier in the book, we recommended that the treatment modules be used in the order presented. The reason for this is that each skill area builds on what has been taught earlier. Optimal use of the program involves an understanding of the ways in which the various skill areas reinforce each other, so that earlier topics can be reviewed and refined as the child's skill repertoire broadens. The following discussion is intended to clarify the interrelationships among the treatment modules.

The program begins with training in *social problem solving*. The goal of this module is to encourage the child to adopt a problem-solving perspective for use in all areas of life, whether it be a conflict with a classmate or problem of low self-esteem. Children are taught a strategy for dealing with difficult situations which arise in everyday life; this should increase their feelings of competence and efficacy as increasingly autonomous individuals. Although none of us feels that we have the solution to every problem we encounter, it is heartening to know that we possess the means by which to arrive at a solution when necessary. This chapter also addresses elementary feeling identification, which is further elaborated in chapter 10, and involves the use of adaptive social and communication skills, which are handled in chapters 10 (Social Understanding and Skills) and 11 (Communication Skills).

A problem-solving perspective is valuable in working on *self-statements*, the module in chapter 6. The child's active participation is required in order to identify and modify problematic self-statements. Since these are private experiences, the counselor can help children devise strategies for accessing and changing their thoughts, but the children themselves must carry out the work. Skillful feeling identification is useful here as well, because feelings can signal the use of adaptive versus problematic self-statements.

Attributional style (chapter 7) is essentially a special type of self-statement. Here, self-statements are used to explain events, both positive and negative. The skills developed in the identification and modification of self-statements are the same as those needed to address problems with attributional style. Problem-solving skills also are useful in the process of creating and adopting alternative attributions. Again, feelings serve as an important marker of areas which should be targeted for intervention.

Although self-statements and attributional style are essentially cognitive activities, these cognitions may have an effect on the child's behavior. It is the relationship between cognition and behavior which is addressed in the module on *self-control* (chapter 8). In this area, cognitive strategies are taught for the goal of affecting the child's outward behavior. This may be seen as creating new self-statements. The processes of making plans and envisioning the consequences of certain behaviors are components of problem solving, and are reintroduced here to help children control their own behavior.

The link between cognitions and behavior is emphasized again in the section on *standard setting* (chapter 8), where children's cognitive evaluation of their behavioral performance is addressed. The use of self-statements and attributions is explicitly incorporated in this module. By now, children should be skilled in monitoring and reporting their thoughts and feelings, and modifying these thoughts should be becoming more familiar as well. In addition to making changes in children's thoughts, the stage is being set for changing behavior. Increasing children's success in self-control teaches them that planned cognitive activity can bring internal standards and external behavior into closer alignment; similarly, the next two chapters will concentrate on changing behavior through increased understanding of self and others, thereby enhancing children's ability to bring their performance up to a desired level.

The module on *social understanding and skills* (chapter 10) uses children's previously learned abilities to inspect their own thoughts and feelings in order to develop the more sophisticated ability to discern the thoughts and feelings of others. These efforts to develop social sensitivity are directly related to the ability to successfully use the *communication skills* taught in the next module (chapter 11). Skillful communication relies heavily on the ability to monitor one's own thoughts and feelings while staying tuned to the internal experiences of others. Once this complex package of skills is acquired, children have many of the necessary tools to function effectively with others and to feel good about doing so.

In the final intervention chapter, chapter 12, the area of *body image* is addressed to illustrate the use of the program with one specific component of self-esteem. Various cognitive strategies, described in previous chapters, are applied to helping children learn to accept their physical selves. In a similar fashion, the elements of the program can be used with self-esteem deficits in other areas, such as social or academic performance. This chapter serves as a reminder that the teaching of new cognitive and behavioral skills must be meaningfully tied to specific areas of children's lives in order to be useful outside of sessions.

It should be clear by now that the cognitive, affective, behavioral, and physical skills described in the treatment program are interdependent. The most successful application of the program will make use of newly acquired abilities to enhance performance in other areas. For just as self-esteem has many interrelated aspects, so must intervention efforts attempt to exert an impact upon the self-image from many coordinated perspectives.

References

Abramson, L. Y., Seligman, M. E. P., & Teasdale, J. (1978). Learned helplessness in humans: Critique and reformulation. *Journal of Abnormal Psychology, 87*, 49–74.

American Psychiatric Association (1987). *Diagnostic and statistical manual of mental disorders* (3rd ed.—revised). Washington, DC: American Psychiatric Association.

Ames, R. (1957). Physical maturing among boys as related to adult social behavior: A longitudinal study. *California Journal of Educational Research, 8*, 69–75.

Asher, S. (1978). Children's peer relations. In M. Lamb (Ed.), *Sociopersonality development.* New York: Holt.

Bernstein, D. A., & Borkovec, T. D. (1973). *Progressive relaxation: A manual for therapists.* Champaign, IL: Research Press.

Bierman, K. L. (1983). Cognitive development and clinical interviews with children. In B. B. Lahay and A. E. Kazdin (eds.) *Advances in clinical child psychology* (6). New York: Plenum.

Canfield, J., & Wells, H. C. (1976). *100 ways to enhance self-concept in the classroom: A handbook for teachers and parents.* Englewood Cliffs, NJ: Prentice-Hall.

Clabby, J. F., & Elias, M. J. (1986). *Teach your child decision making.* New York: Doubleday.

Cooley, C. (1962). *Human nature and the social order.* New York: Charles Scribner's Sons.

Craighead, L. W., & Green, B. J. (1987). The relationship between depression and sex-typed personality characteristics in adolescents. Unpublished manuscript. University of North Carolina, Chapel Hill, NC.

Craighead, W. E., Meyers, A. W., & Craighead, L. W. (1985). A conceptual model for cognitive-behavior therapy with children. *Journal of Abnormal Child Psychology, 13*(3), 331–342.

Dion, K., Berscheid, E., & Walster, E. (1972). What is beautiful is good. *Journal of Personality and Social Psychology, 24*, 285–290.

Dodge, K., & Frame, C. (1982). Social cognitive biases and deficits in aggressive boys. *Child Development, 53*, 620–635.

Dornbusch, S., Carlsmith, J., Duncan, P., Gross, R., Marto, J., Ritter, P., Siegel-Gorelick, B. (1984). Sexual maturation, social class, and the desire to be thin among adolescent females. *Developmental and Behavioral Pediatrics, 5*, 308–314.

D'Zurilla, T. J., & Goldfried, M. R. (1971). Problem solving and behavior modification. *Journal of Abnormal Psychology, 78*, 107–126.

Eating Disorders 'Normal.' (1985, November.) *APA Monitor*, p. 14.

Elias, M. J. (1981). Adolescent Self and Context Measure: Form ASCM-M81. Unpublished assessment procedure, Rutgers University, New Brunswick, NJ.

Elkind, D. (1978). Understanding the young adolescent. *Adolescence*, Spring, 127–134.

Epstein, S. (1973). The self-concept revisited or a theory of a theory. *American Psychologist, 28*, 405–416.

Flavell, J. (1985). *Cognitive development*: Englewood Cliffs, NJ: Prentice-Hall.

Gottman, J. M., Gonso, J., & Rasmussen, B. (1975). Social interaction, social competence, and friendship in children. *Child Development, 46*, 709–718.

Harter, S. (1983). Developmental perspectives on the self system. In E. M. Hetherington (Ed.). *Handbook of child psychology: Socialization personality and social development* (Vol. 4). New York: Wiley.

Harter, S. (1985). Manual for the self-perception profile for children (revision of the perceived competence scale for children). Unpublished manuscript, University of Denver, Denver, Co.

James, W. (1890). *Principles of Psychology*. New York: Holt.

Jones, M. (1965). Psychological correlates of somatic development. *Child Development, 36*, 899–911.

Jones, M., & Bayley, N. (1950). Physical maturing among boys as related to behavior. *Journal of Educational Psychology, 41*, 129–148.

Kagan, J., Rosman, B., Day, D., Albert, J., & Phillips, W. (1964). Information processing in the child: Significance of analytic and reflective attitudes. *Psychological Monographs*, (Whole No. 578).

Kanfer, F. H. (1970). Self-regulation: Research, issues, and speculations. In C. Neuringer & J. L. Michael (Eds.), *Behavior modification in clinical psychology* (pp. 178–220). New York: Appleton.

Kanfer, F. H. (1971). The maintenance of behaviors by self-generated stimuli and reinforcement. In A. Jacobs & L. B. Sachs (Eds.). The psychology of private events: Perspectives on covert response systems (pp. 39–59). New York: Academic.

Keller, A., Ford, L., & Meacham, J. (1978). Dimensions of self-concept in preschool children. *Developmental Psychology, 14*, 483–489.

Kohlberg, L. (1966). A cognitive-developmental analysis of children's sex-role concepts and attitudes. In E. Maccoby (Ed.), *The development of sex differences*: Stanford, CA: Stanford University Press.

Kohlberg, L. (1969). *Stages in the development of moral thought and action*. New York: Holt.

Krauss, R., & Glucksberg, F. (1977). Social and nonsocial speech. *Scientific American, 236*, 100–105.

Ladd, G. (1981). Effectiveness of a social learning method for enhancing children's social interaction and peer acceptance. *Child Development, 52*, 171–178.

Lepper, M. (1981). Intrinsic and extrinsic motivation in children: Detrimental effects of superfluous social controls. In W. Collins (Ed.), *Aspects of the development of competence: The Minnesota symposium on child psychology* (Vol. 14). Hillsdale, NJ: Lawrence Erlbaum.

Lerner, R., Busch-Rossnagel, N. (1981). Individuals as producers of their development: Conceptual and empirical bases. In R. M. Lerner & N. Busch-Rossnagel (Eds.), *Individuals as producers of their development: A life-span perspective*. New York: Academic Press.

Lerner, R., Karabenick, S., & Stuart, J. (1973). Relations among physical attractiveness, body attitudes, and self-concept in male and female college students. *Journal of Psychology, 85*, 119–129.

Lerner, R., Orlos, J., & Knapp, J. (1976). Physical attractiveness, physical effectiveness, and self-concept in late adolescence. *Adolescent, 11*, 313–326.

Livesley, W., & Bromley, D. (1973). *Person perception in childhood and adolescence*. London: Wiley.

Loevinger, J. (1966). The meaning and measure of ego development. *American Psychologist, 21*, 195–206.

Loevinger, J. (1976). *Ego development: Conceptions and theories*. San Francisco: Jossey-Bass.

Loevinger, J., & Wessler, R. (1970). *Measuring ego development* (Vol. 1). San Francisco: Jossey-Bass.

Luria, A. (1961). *The role of speech in the regulation of normal and abnormal behaviors*. New York: Liveright.

Maccoby, E., & Martin, J. (1983). Socialization in the context of the family. In E. Hetherington (Ed.), *Handbook of child psychology; Socialization, personality, and social development* (Vol. 4). New York: Wiley.

Magnusson, D., Stattin, H., & Allen, V. (1985). Biological maturation and social development: A longitudinal study of some adjustment processes from mid-adolescence to adulthood. *Journal of Youth and Adolescence, 14*, 267–282.

Meacham, J. (1979). The role of verbal activity in remembering the goals of actions. In G. Zivin (Ed.), *The development of self-regulation through private speech* (pp. 237–264). New York: Wiley.

Mead, G. (1934). *Mind, self, and society*. Chicago: University of Chicago Press.

Mussen, P., & Jones, M. (1957). Self-conceptions, motivations, and interpersonal attitudes of late- and early-maturing boys. *Child Development, 28*, 249–256.

Novaco, R. (1978). Anger and coping with stress. In J. Foreyt & D. Rathjen (Eds.), *Cognitive behavior therapy* (pp. 135–173). New York: Plenum.

New Options. (1986, April 28). Political priority #1: Teaching kids to like themselves. *New Options*, p. 1.

Parke, R. (1969). Effectiveness of punishment as an interaction of intensity, timing, agent nurturance and cognitive-structuring. *Child Development, 40*, 213–235.

Peevers, B., & Secord, P. (1973). Development changes in attribution of descriptive concepts to persons. *Journal of Personality and Social Psychology, 27*, 120–128.

Peterson, C., & Seligman, M. E. P. (1984). Causal explanations as a risk factor for depression: Theory and evidence. *Psychological Review, 91*, 347–374.

Piaget, J. (1932). *The moral judgement of the child*. New York: Harcourt, Brace.

Piers, E. V. (1976). *The Piers-Harris children's self-concept scale: Research monograph #1*. Nashville, TN: Counselor Recordings and Tests.

Pressley, M. (1979). Increasing children's self-control through cognitive interventions. *Review of Education Research, 49*, 319–370.

Putallaz, M., & Gottman, J. (1981). Social skills and group acceptance. In S. Asher & J. Gottman (Eds.), *The development of children's friendships*. Cambridge: Cambridge University Press.

Rosen, G., & Ross, A. (1968). Relationship of body image to self-concept. *Journal of Consulting and Clinical Psychology, 32*, 100.

Rosenberg, M. (1979). *Conceiving the self*. New York: Basic Books.

Ruble, D., Boggiano, A., Feldman, N., & Loebl, J. (1980). Developmental analysis of the role of social comparison in self-evaluation. *Developmental Psychology, 16*, 105–115.

Sacco, W. P. & Beck, A. T. (1985). Cognitive therapy of depression. In E. E. Beckham & W. R. Leber (Eds.), *Handbook of depression: Treatment, assessment, and research* (pp. 3–38). Homewood, IL: Dorsey.

Secord, P., & Jourard, S. (1953). The appraisal of body cathexis and self. *Journal of Consulting Psychology, 17*, 343–347.

Seligman, M. E. P., & Peterson C. (1986). A learned helplessness perspective on childhood depression: Theory and research. In M. Rutter, C. E. Izard, & P. B. Read (Eds.), *Depression in young people: Developmental and clinical perspectives* (pp. 223–249). New York: Guilford.

Selman, R. (1976). Social-cognitive understanding: A guide to educational and clinical practice. In T. Lickona (Ed.), *Moral development and behavior* (pp. 299–316). New York: Holt, Rinehart, & Winston.

Shantz, C. (1975). The development of social cognition. In E. M. Hetherington (Ed.), *Review of child development research* (Vol. 5). Chicago: University of Chicago Press.

Shantz, C. (1983). Social cognition. In J. Flavell & E. Markman (Eds.), *Handbook of child psychology: Cognitive development* (Vol. 3). New York: Wiley.

Simmons, R. G., & Blyth, D. A. (In press). *Moving into adolescence: The impact of pubertal change and school context*. New York: Aldine.

Weatherly, D. (1964). Self-perceived rate of physical maturation and personality in late adolescence. *Child Development, 35,* 1197–1210.

Zajonc, R. (1980). Feelings and thinking. *American Psychologist, 35,* 151–175.

Zakin, D., Blyth, D., Simmons, R. (1984). Physical attractiveness as a mediator of the impact of early pubertal changes for girls. *Journal of Youth and Adolescence, 13,* 439–451.

Appendix 4.1

Scoring for the Five-Scale Test of Self-Esteem for Children

SCORE   Almost Always = 2
           Sometimes = 1
           Almost Never = 0

(Note: Items in parentheses below should be scored in reverse, i.e., Almost Always = 0, Sometimes = 1, Almost Never = 2.)

SUBSCALES

Global Scale
Items 1, 7, (13), (19), 25, 31, 37, (43), (49), (55)

Academic Scale
Items (2), 8, (14), 20, (26), 32, (38), 44, (50), 56

Body Scale
Items (3), 9, (16), 21, (27), 33, (39), 45, (51), 57

Family Scale
Items 4, 10, (16), (22), 28, 34, 40, (46), (52), (58)

Social Scale
Items (5), (11), 17, 23, (29), (35), (41), 47, 53, 59

Lie Scale
Items 6, (12), (18), (24), 30, 36, 42, (48), 54, (60)

(Note: A score of 2 (Almost Always) on four or more items of the Lie Scale suggests that the child may be responding in a socially desirable manner and consequently, the validity of the self-esteem scales may be in question.)

☐ BOY   ☐ GIRL

THESE QUESTIONS ARE TO HELP US LEARN ABOUT HOW BOYS AND GIRLS YOUR AGE FEEL ABOUT DIFFERENT THINGS.

THERE ARE NO RIGHT OR WRONG ANSWERS. ONLY YOU KNOW YOUR REAL FEELINGS. IT IS IMPORTANT THAT YOU ANSWER THE WAY YOU *REALLY* FEEL, NOT HOW SOMEBODY ELSE THINKS YOU SHOULD FEEL.

EXAMPLE:

	I FEEL THIS WAY:		
a. I like to read.	ALMOST ALWAYS	SOMETIMES	ALMOST NEVER

NAME _____

GRADE _____

1. I like most things about myself.	I FEEL THIS WAY: ALMOST ALWAYS SOMETIMES	ALMOST NEVER
2. I'm disappointed with my school grades.	I FEEL THIS WAY: ALMOST ALWAYS SOMETIMES	ALMOST NEVER
3. I am too clumsy.	I FEEL THIS WAY: ALMOST ALWAYS SOMETIMES	ALMOST NEVER
4. I am an important member of my family.	I FEEL THIS WAY: ALMOST ALWAYS SOMETIMES	ALMOST NEVER
5. I worry about other kids liking me.	I FEEL THIS WAY: ALMOST ALWAYS SOMETIMES	ALMOST NEVER
6. I do some homework every day of the week.	I FEEL THIS WAY: ALMOST ALWAYS SOMETIMES	ALMOST NEVER
7. I'm an important person.	I FEEL THIS WAY: ALMOST ALWAYS SOMETIMES	ALMOST NEVER
8. I'm good enough at reading.	I FEEL THIS WAY: ALMOST ALWAYS SOMETIMES	ALMOST NEVER
9. I like the way I look.	I FEEL THIS WAY: ALMOST ALWAYS SOMETIMES	ALMOST NEVER
10. I feel good about myself when I'm with my family.	I FEEL THIS WAY: ALMOST ALWAYS SOMETIMES	ALMOST NEVER
11. Other kids make me feel like I'm not good enough.	I FEEL THIS WAY: ALMOST ALWAYS SOMETIMES	ALMOST NEVER
12. I say things that are not true.	I FEEL THIS WAY: ALMOST ALWAYS SOMETIMES	ALMOST NEVER

13. I wish I were somebody else.	I FEEL THIS WAY: ALMOST ALWAYS SOMETIMES ALMOST NEVER
14. I wish I understood more when the teacher explains things.	I FEEL THIS WAY: ALMOST ALWAYS SOMETIMES ALMOST NEVER
15. I wish my height were more like other kids my age.	I FEEL THIS WAY: ALMOST ALWAYS SOMETIMES ALMOST NEVER
16. I feel like running away from home.	I FEEL THIS WAY: ALMOST ALWAYS SOMETIMES ALMOST NEVER
17. My friends listen to my ideas.	I FEEL THIS WAY: ALMOST ALWAYS SOMETIMES ALMOST NEVER
18. It doesn't bother me when I lose a game.	I FEEL THIS WAY: ALMOST ALWAYS SOMETIMES ALMOST NEVER
19. I have a low opinion of myself.	I FEEL THIS WAY: ALMOST ALWAYS SOMETIMES ALMOST NEVER
20. I'm proud of the work I do in school.	I FEEL THIS WAY: ALMOST ALWAYS SOMETIMES ALMOST NEVER
21. I have a nice face.	I FEEL THIS WAY: ALMOST ALWAYS SOMETIMES ALMOST NEVER
22. I make my parents unhappy.	I FEEL THIS WAY: ALMOST ALWAYS SOMETIMES ALMOST NEVER
23. I feel good about myself when I'm with my friends.	I FEEL THIS WAY: ALMOST ALWAYS SOMETIMES ALMOST NEVER
24. If I got mad at a friend, I might call him a name.	I FEEL THIS WAY: ALMOST ALWAYS SOMETIMES ALMOST NEVER

25. I'm an interesting person.	I FEEL THIS WAY: ALMOST ALWAYS SOMETIMES	ALMOST NEVER
26. I'm too slow at finishing my schoolwork.	I FEEL THIS WAY: ALMOST ALWAYS SOMETIMES	ALMOST NEVER
27. I would like my weight to be different.	I FEEL THIS WAY: ALMOST ALWAYS SOMETIMES	ALMOST NEVER
28. I am a good daughter/son.	I FEEL THIS WAY: ALMOST ALWAYS SOMETIMES	ALMOST NEVER
29. I am lonely.	I FEEL THIS WAY: ALMOST ALWAYS SOMETIMES	ALMOST NEVER
30. I make my bed in the morning without being reminded.	I FEEL THIS WAY: ALMOST ALWAYS SOMETIMES	ALMOST NEVER
31. I am a good person.	I FEEL THIS WAY: ALMOST ALWAYS SOMETIMES	ALMOST NEVER
32. I feel good about myself when I'm at school.	I FEEL THIS WAY: ALMOST ALWAYS SOMETIMES	ALMOST NEVER
33. I have a nice smile.	I FEEL THIS WAY: ALMOST ALWAYS SOMETIMES	ALMOST NEVER
34. My parents have good reason to be proud of me.	I FEEL THIS WAY: ALMOST ALWAYS SOMETIMES	ALMOST NEVER
35. I wish I were better at making friends.	I FEEL THIS WAY: ALMOST ALWAYS SOMETIMES	ALMOST NEVER
36. If I really want to win a game, I might break a rule.	I FEEL THIS WAY: ALMOST ALWAYS SOMETIMES	ALMOST NEVER

37. I'm happy with the way I am.	I FEEL THIS WAY: ALMOST ALMOST ALWAYS SOMETIMES NEVER
38. I am dumb at school work.	I FEEL THIS WAY: ALMOST ALMOST ALWAYS SOMETIMES NEVER
39. I feel bad about the way I look.	I FEEL THIS WAY: ALMOST ALMOST ALWAYS SOMETIMES NEVER
40. I have one of the best families in the whole world.	I FEEL THIS WAY: ALMOST ALMOST ALWAYS SOMETIMES NEVER
41. I wish I had friends who really liked me.	I FEEL THIS WAY: ALMOST ALMOST ALWAYS SOMETIMES NEVER
42. I go to bed without complaining when it's my bedtime.	I FEEL THIS WAY: ALMOST ALMOST ALWAYS SOMETIMES NEVER
43. I'm not good at things.	I FEEL THIS WAY: ALMOST ALMOST ALWAYS SOMETIMES NEVER
44. I think my report cards are good enough.	I FEEL THIS WAY: ALMOST ALMOST ALWAYS SOMETIMES NEVER
45. I am OK at the sports and games I like to play.	I FEEL THIS WAY: ALMOST ALMOST ALWAYS SOMETIMES NEVER
46. My family is disappointed in me.	I FEEL THIS WAY: ALMOST ALMOST ALWAYS SOMETIMES NEVER
47. I can make friends when I want to.	I FEEL THIS WAY: ALMOST ALMOST ALWAYS SOMETIMES NEVER
48. I get angry when my parents won't let me do something I really want to.	I FEEL THIS WAY: ALMOST ALMOST ALWAYS SOMETIMES NEVER

	I FEEL THIS WAY:
49. I feel like a failure.	ALMOST ALWAYS SOMETIMES ALMOST NEVER
50. I wish I were a better student.	I FEEL THIS WAY: ALMOST ALWAYS SOMETIMES ALMOST NEVER
51. I would like to look like somebody else.	I FEEL THIS WAY: ALMOST ALWAYS SOMETIMES ALMOST NEVER
52. I think my parents would be happy if I were a lot different.	I FEEL THIS WAY: ALMOST ALWAYS SOMETIMES ALMOST NEVER
53. I have enough friends.	I FEEL THIS WAY: ALMOST ALWAYS SOMETIMES ALMOST NEVER
54. I brush my teeth after every meal.	I FEEL THIS WAY: ALMOST ALWAYS SOMETIMES ALMOST NEVER
55. I'm not proud of anything about myself.	I FEEL THIS WAY: ALMOST ALWAYS SOMETIMES ALMOST NEVER
56. I'm good enough at arithmetic.	I FEEL THIS WAY: ALMOST ALWAYS SOMETIMES ALMOST NEVER
57. I have a nice body build.	I FEEL THIS WAY: ALMOST ALWAYS SOMETIMES ALMOST NEVER
58. I don't like the way I act when I'm with my family.	I FEEL THIS WAY: ALMOST ALWAYS SOMETIMES ALMOST NEVER
59. I am a good friend.	I FEEL THIS WAY: ALMOST ALWAYS SOMETIMES ALMOST NEVER
60. I would let somebody else take the blame for something I did wrong.	I FEEL THIS WAY: ALMOST ALWAYS SOMETIMES ALMOST NEVER

Appendix 4.2

Checklist for Compiling Self-Esteem Data

Global   Yes   No
1. Does the child approach new situations with confidence?
2. Are important adults (teachers, parents) generally positive
   in their comments about the child?
3. Does the child avoid self-critical statements?

Academic
1. Does the child feel satisfied with her academic
   performance?
2. Can the child differentiate areas of strength and weakness
   and feel comfortable with each?
3. Is the child able to set reasonable standards for her
   performance so that she regularly experiences success?

Social
1. Is the child satisfied with the quantity and quality of his
   peer relationships?
2. Does the child possess the skills he needs to pursue the
   social contacts he desires?
3. Does the child have at least one or two friends by whom
   he feels liked and accepted?

Body
1. Is the child satisfied with her appearance?
2. Is the child satisfied with the performance of his body in
   sports and activities he enjoys?
3. Are peers accepting of the child's physical appearance and
   abilities?

Family
1. Does the child feel like a valued member of her family?
2. Are the child's parents accepting of the whole child (even if they point out areas which require change)?
3. Does the child feel good about himself when he is with his family?

Appendix 13.1
Bibliography of Skills Training Programs

Camp, B. W., & Bash, M. S. (1985). *Think aloud: Increasing social and cognitive skills—a problem-solving program for children.* Champaign, IL: Research Press.

Geared toward early elementary-age children, a self-control program using problem solving approach.

Goldstein, A., & Keller, H. (1987). *Aggressive behavior: Assessment and intervention.* New York: Pergamon.

Includes techniques for developing self-control with children who have difficulty controlling anger and aggressive behavior.

Goldstein, A., Sprafkin, R., Gershaw, N., & Klein, P. (1980). *Skill-streaming the adolescent: A structured learning approach to teaching prosocial skills.* Champaign, IL: Research Press.

The skill-streaming books provide a step-by-step guide for teaching social skills applicable to classroom and peer relations.

Kendall, P., & Braswell, L. (1985). *Cognitive–behavioral therapy for impulsive children.* New York: Guilford.

For impulsive and aggressive children and adolescents, a self-control program applied to academic and social areas.

McGinnis, E., & Goldstein, A. (1984). *Skill-streaming the elementary school child: A guide for teaching prosocial skills.* Champaign, IL: Research Press.

Santostefano, S. (1985). *Cognitive control therapy with children and adolescents.* New York: Pergamon.

A self-control program focusing on the development of cognitive skills for children with learning dysfunctions.

Author Index

Subject Index

About the Authors

Dr. Alice W. Pope is a post-doctoral research fellow in Child Psychiatry at the Schneider Children's Hospital of Long Island Jewish Medical Center. She received her PhD in child clinical psychology from The Pennsylvania State University in 1986. Her research interests involve children's peer relationships, with a particular emphasis on identifying the characteristics of children who have difficulty making friends.

Dr. Susan M. McHale is Associate Professor of Human Development in the College of Human Development at The Pennsylvania State University. She received her PhD in Developmental Psychology from the University of North Carolina at Chapel Hill in 1979. Her research interests focus on children's interpersonal relationships—particularly family relationships—how they develop and how they are related to children's psychological well-being.

Dr. W. Edward Craighead is a Professor in the Division of Medical Psychology in the Department of Psychiatry at Duke University Medical Center. He received his PhD in 1970 from the University of Illinois at Urbana–Champaign, and he was a member of the faculty of the Department of Psychology at The Pennsylvania State University from 1970–1986. His research includes studies of depression and affective disorders over the lifespan.

Psychology Practitioner Guidebooks

Editor
Arnold P. Goldstein, Syracuse University
Leonard Krasner, Stanford University & SUNY at Stony Brook
Sol. L. Garfield, Washington University in St. Louis

Elsie M. Pinkston & Nathan L. Linsk — CARE OF THE ELDERLY: A Family Approach

Donald Meichenbaum — STRESS INOCULATION TRAINING

Sebastiano Santostefano — COGNITIVE CONTROL THERAPY WITH CHILDREN AND ADOLESCENTS

Lillie Weiss, Melanie Katzman & Sharlene Wolchik — TREATING BULIMIA: A Psychoeducational Approach

Edward B. Blanchard & Frank Andrasik — MANAGEMENT OF CHRONIC HEADACHES: A Psychological Approach

Raymond G. Romanczyk — CLINICAL UTILIZATION OF MICRO-COMPUTER TECHNOLOGY

Philip H. Bornstein & Marcy T. Bornstein — MARITAL THERAPY: A Behavioral-Communications Approach

Michael T. Nietzel & Ronald C. Dillehay — PSYCHOLOGICAL CONSULTATION IN THE COURTROOM

Elizabeth B. Yost, Larry E. Beutler, M. Anne Corbishley & James R. Allender — GROUP COGNITIVE THERAPY: A Treatment Method for Depressed Older Adults

Lillie Weiss — DREAM ANALYSIS IN PSYCHOTHERAPY

Edward A. Kirby & Liam K. Grimley — UNDERSTANDING AND TREATING ATTENTION DEFICIT DISORDER

Jon Eisenson — LANGUAGE AND SPEECH DISORDERS IN CHILDREN

Eva L. Feindler & Randolph B. Ecton — ADOLESCENT ANGER CONTROL: Cognitive-Behavioral Techniques

Michael C. Roberts — PEDIATRIC PSYCHOLOGY: Psychological Interventions and Strategies for Pediatric Problems

Daniel S. Kirschenbaum, William G. Johnson & Peter M. Stalonas, Jr. — TREATING CHILDHOOD AND ADOLESCENT OBESITY

W. Stewart Agras — EATING DISORDERS: Management of Obesity, Bulimia and Anorexia Nervosa

Ian H. Gotlib & Catherine A. Colby — TREATMENT OF DEPRESSION: An Interpersonal Systems Approach

Walter B. Pryzwansky & Robert N. Wendt — PSYCHOLOGY AS A PROFESSION: Foundations of Practice

Cynthia D. Belar, William W. Deardorff & Karen E. Kelly — THE PRACTICE OF CLINICAL HEALTH PSYCHOLOGY

Paul Karoly & Mark P. Jensen — MULTIMETHOD ASSESSMENT OF CHRONIC PAIN

William L. Golden, E. Thomas Dowd & Fred Friedberg — HYPNOTHERAPY: A Modern Approach

Patricia Lacks — BEHAVIORAL TREATMENT FOR PERSISTENT INSOMNIA

Arnold P. Goldstein & Harold Keller — AGGRESSIVE BEHAVIOR: Assessment and Intervention

C. Eugene Walker, Barbara L. Bonner & Keith L. Kaufman — THE PHYSICALLY AND SEXUALLY ABUSED CHILD: Evaluation and Treatment

Robert E. Becker, Richard G. Heimberg & Alan S. Bellack — SOCIAL SKILLS TRAINING TREATMENT FOR DEPRESSION

Richard F. Dangel & Richard A. Polster — TEACHING CHILD MANAGEMENT SKILLS

Albert Ellis, John F. McInerney, Raymond DiGiuseppe & Raymond Yeager — RATIONAL-EMOTIVE THERAPY WITH ALCOHOLICS AND SUBSTANCE ABUSERS

Johnny L. Matson & Thomas H. Ollendick — ENHANCING CHILDREN'S SOCIAL SKILLS: Assessment and Training

Edward B. Blanchard, John E. Martin & Patricia M. Dubbert — NON-DRUG TREATMENTS FOR ESSENTIAL HYPERTENSION

Samuel M. Turner & Deborah C. Beidel — TREATING OBSESSIVE-COMPULSIVE DISORDER

Alice W. Pope, Susan M. McHale & W. Edward Craighead — SELF-ESTEEM ENHANCEMENT WITH CHILDREN AND ADOLESCENTS

Jean E. Rhodes & Leonard A. Jason — PREVENTING SUBSTANCE ABUSE AMONG CHILDREN AND ADOLESCENTS

Gerald D. Oster, Janice E. Caro, Daniel R. Eagen & Margaret A. Lillo — ASSESSING ADOLESCENTS